Marx Joyce Abbott Hardy Machiavelli Montaigne Chesterton Cooper Emerson Austen Defoe Melville Haggard Hugo Eliot Grimm Christie Carroll Stoker Molière Wilde Byron Maupassant Schiller Engels Garnett Einstein Fitzgerald Hawthorne Smith Kafka Goethe Dostoyevsky Cotton Hall Baum Kipling Doyle Willis Henry Leslie Dumas Nietzsche Flaubert Turgenev Balzac Stockton Vatsyayana Crane Burroughs Verne Curtis Tocqueville Whitman Gogol Vinci Homer Widger Tolstoy Busch Darwin Thoreau Potter Freud Zola Twain Plato Scott Lawrence Kant Jowett Stevenson Dickens Andersen Burton Hesse Harte London Descartes Cervantes Poe Aristotle Wells Voltaire Hale James Hastings Cooke Bunner Shakespeare Richter Chekhov da Chambers Irving Doré Swift Dante Shaw Wodehouse Benedict Alcott Pushkin Newton tredition®

tredition was established in 2006 by Sandra Latusseck and Soenke Schulz. Based in Hamburg, Germany, tredition offers publishing solutions to authors and publishing houses, combined with worldwide distribution of printed and digital book content. tredition is uniquely positioned to enable authors and publishing houses to create books on their own terms and without conventional manufacturing risks.

For more information please visit: www.tredition.com

TREDITION CLASSICS

This book is part of the TREDITION CLASSICS series. The creators of this series are united by passion for literature and driven by the intention of making all public domain books available in printed format again - worldwide. Most TREDITION CLASSICS titles have been out of print and off the bookstore shelves for decades. At tredition we believe that a great book never goes out of style and that its value is eternal. Several mostly non-profit literature projects provide content to tredition. To support their good work, tredition donates a portion of the proceeds from each sold copy. As a reader of a TREDITION CLASSICS book, you support our mission to save many of the amazing works of world literature from oblivion. See all available books at www.tredition.com.

Project Gutenberg

The content for this book has been graciously provided by Project Gutenberg. Project Gutenberg is a non-profit organization founded by Michael Hart in 1971 at the University of Illinois. The mission of Project Gutenberg is simple: To encourage the creation and distribution of eBooks. Project Gutenberg is the first and largest collection of public domain eBooks.

Communism and Christianism Analyzed and Contrasted from the Marxian and Darwinian Points of View

William Montgomery Brown

Imprint

This book is part of TREDITION CLASSICS

Author: William Montgomery Brown
Cover design: Buchgut, Berlin – Germany

Publisher: tredition GmbH, Hamburg - Germany
ISBN: 978-3-8472-1943-9

www.tredition.com
www.tredition.de

The intention of the TREDITION CLASSICS series is to make world literature in the public domain available in printed format. Literary enthusiasts and organizations, such as Project Gutenberg, worldwide have scanned and digitally edited the original texts. tredition has subsequently formatted and redesigned the content into a modern reading layout. Therefore, we cannot guarantee the exact reproduction of the original format of a particular historic edition. Please also note that no modifications have been made to the spelling, therefore it may differ from the orthography used today.

To the Purchaser:

Lying Supernaturalism is going; robbing Capitalism is falling; saving Laborism is rising, and leveling Unionism is coming.

This booklet, Communism and Christianism, is a contribution by Bishop and Mrs. Wm. M. Brown, of Galion, Ohio, towards the furtherance of these downward, upward and forward movements, the most fortunate events in the whole history of mankind. We hope that you will read, mark, learn and inwardly digest its extremely revolutionary, comprehensive and salutary teachings concerning both religion and politics with the happy result of becoming an apostle of its illuminating and inspiring interpretation of the scientific gospel of Marx and Engels to wage slaves, the only gospel which points the way to redemption from their body and soul destroying slavery.

You may become a missionary of this gospel in your neighborhood, and as such do more good than all its orthodox preachers, teachers, editors and politicians together at no financial cost to yourself by ordering booklets at our special rates: six copies, $1.00; twenty-five copies, $3.00, prepaid, and selling them to workers at our retail price, 25 cents for one copy. As we make no profit and do no bookkeeping, cash should accompany all orders.

To organizations working for bail, defense, liberation or unemployment funds, Bishop and Mrs. Brown donate twenty-five copies for each twenty-five ordered with remittance.

The Bradford-Brown Educational Company, Inc. Publishers—Galion, Ohio

Editions and Their Dates.

First Edition, 10,000 copies, October 11th, 1920.

Second Edition, 10,000 copies, revised and enlarged from 184 to 204 pages, February 15th, 1921.

Third Edition, 10,000 copies, March 2nd, 1921.

Fourth Edition, 10,000 copies (2,000 in cloth binding), revised and enlarged from 204 to 224 pages, April 9, 1921.

Rt. Rev. William Montgomery Brown, D. D.
Fifth Bishop of Arkansas, Resigned; Member House of Bishops Protestant Episcopal Church; Sometime Archdeacon of Ohio and Special Lecturer at Bexley Hall, the Theological Seminary of Kenyon College. Now Episcopos in partibus Bolshevikium et Infidelium.

COMMUNISM AND CHRISTIANISM

ANALYZED AND CONTRASTED FROM THE MARXIAN AND DARWINIAN POINTS OF VIEW

by

William Montgomery Brown

Banish the Gods from the Skies
and Capitalists from the
Earth and make the world safe
for Industrial Communism.

The Bradford-Brown Educational Company, Inc. Publishers ...
Galion, Ohio

Fortieth Thousand

DEDICATION

This booklet is gratefully dedicated to the Proletariat from whom Bishop and Mrs. Brown are sprung, and to whose unrequited labors (not to the good providence of a divinity) they owe their wealth, leisure and opportunities.

[Pg 5]

PROLEGOMENA [A]

Religion is the opium of the people. The suppression of religion as the happiness of the people is the revindication of its real happiness. The invitation to abandon illusions regarding its situation is an invitation to abandon a situation which has need of illusions. Criticism of religion is therefore the germ of a criticism of the vale of tears, of which religion is the holy aspect.

—Marx.

Not only, indeed, is the struggle against religion intellectually useful, but it cannot conscientiously be avoided, for religion is used against the Socialist movement by the possessing class in every country.

But to abolish religion is not to abolish exploitation, because only one of the enemy's guns will have been silenced. The workers have, above all, to dislodge the capitalist class from power. The religious question, and indeed all else, is secondary to this.

The test of admission to a Socialist Party must be neither more nor less than acceptance of the following seven working principles and the policy of Socialism as a class movement:

1. Society as at present constituted is based upon the ownership of the means of living (i. e., land, factories, railways, etc.) by the capitalist or master class, and the consequent enslavement of the working class, by whose labor alone wealth is produced.

[Pg 6]

2. In society, therefore, there is an antagonism of interests, manifesting itself as a class struggle, between those who possess but do not produce and those who produce but do not possess.

3. This antagonism can be abolished only by the emancipation of the working class from the domination of the master class by the conversion into the common property of society of the means of production and distribution, and their democratic control by the whole people.

4. As in the order of social evolution the working class is the last to achieve its freedom, the emancipation of the working class will involve the emancipation of all mankind without distinction of race or sex.

5. This emancipation must be the work of the working class itself.

6. As the machinery of capitalist government, including the armed forces of the nation, conserves the monopoly by the capitalist class of the wealth taken from the workers, the working class must organize consciously and politically for acquiring the powers of government, national and local, in order that this machinery, including these forces, may be converted from an instrument of oppression into the agent of emancipation and the overthrow of privilege, aristocratic and plutocratic. [B]

7. As all political parties are but the expression of class interests, and as the interest of the working class is diametrically opposed to the interests of all sections [Pg 7] of the master-class, the party seeking working-class emancipation must be hostile to every other party.

If a man supports the church, or in any respect allows religious ideas to stand in the way of the foregoing seven essential principles of socialism or the activity of a Party, he proves thereby that he does not accept Socialism as fundamentally true and of the first importance, and his place is outside.

No man can be consistently both a Socialist and a Christian. It must be either the socialist or the religious principle that is supreme, for the attempt to couple them equally betrays charlatanism or lack of thought. There is, therefore, no need for a specifically anti-religious test.

So surely does the acceptance of Socialism lead to the exclusion of the supernatural, that the Socialist has little need for such terms as Atheist, Free-thinker, or even Materialist; for the word Socialist, rightly understood, implies one who, on all such questions, takes his stand on positive science, explaining all things by purely natural causation, Socialism being not merely a politico-economic creed, but also an integral part of a consistent world philosophy.

So long as the anarchy of modern competitive society exists, the accompanying obscurity and confusion in social life will continue to shelter superstition. This point is illustrated in the following reference by Marx to the United States:

When we see in the very country of complete political emancipation not only that religion exists, but retains its vigour, there is no need, I hope, for other proofs in order to show that the existence of religion is not incompatible with the full political maturity of the State. But if religion exists it is be [Pg 8] cause of a defective social organization, of which it is necessary to seek the cause in the very essence of the State.

Class domination is the essence of the modern State. It is based on competitive anarchy and parasitism—the evidences of a defective social organization. It still leaves room for religion, because it maintains ignorance and confusion by its structure and contradictions, and because religion is fostered as a handmaiden of class rule.

Nevertheless, the growth of the social forces of production within modern society, and the better knowledge the workers obtain of their true relations to each other and to Nature, loosen the chains of ghost worship and mysticism from their limbs and lessen the power of religion as a political weapon in the hands of the ruling class, while they form, at the same time, the material and intellectual preparation for an intelligently organized society. The matter has been put in a nutshell by Marx in the chapter on "Commodities" in "Capital," volume I.

The religious reflex of the real world can, in any case, only then finally vanish, when the practical relations of every-day life offer to man none but perfectly intelligible and reasonable relations with regard to his fellow men and to nature.

The life process of society, which is based on the process of material production, does not strip off its mystical veil until it is treated as production by freely associated men, and is consciously regulated by them in accordance with a settled plan.

This, however, demands for society a certain material groundwork or set of conditions of existence which in their turn are the spontaneous product of a long and painful process of development.

[Pg 9]

It is, therefore, a profound truth that Socialism is the natural enemy of religion. Through Socialism alone will the relations between men in society, and their relations to Nature, become reasonable, orderly, and completely intelligible, leaving no nook or cranny for superstition. The entry of Socialism is, consequently, the exodus of religion.

FOOTNOTES:

[A] From the Official Manifesto by the Socialist Party of Great Britain, showing the Antagonism between Socialism and Religion.

[B] This section has been slightly changed to make sure of guarding against the advocacy of armed insurrection. Socialists throughout the world want a peaceful evolution from capitalism into socialism; but whether or not it will be so in the case of any country is, as Lenin prophesies, to be determined by the dealings of its capitalists with its laborers. In reply to an inquiry on this vexed subject by an English author, Lenin said, in effect, that in England, as elsewhere, the tactics of the capitalist class will determine the program of the labor class.

[Pg 10]

THE INTERNATIONAL PARTY.

Arise, ye prisoners of starvation! Arise, ye wretched of the earth, For justice thunders condemnation, A better world's in birth. No more tradition's chains shall bind us, Arise, ye slaves! no more in thrall! The earth shall rise on new foundations, We have been naught, we shall be all.
We want no condescending saviors. To rule us from a judgment hall. We workers ask not for their favors, Let us consult for all. To make the thief disgorge his booty, To free the spirit from its cell, We must ourselves decide our duty, We must decide and do it well.
The law oppresses us and tricks us, Taxation drains the victim's blood; The rich are free from obligations, The laws the poor delude. Too long we've languished in subjection, Equal-

ity has other laws: "No rights," says she, "without their duties. No claims on equals without cause."
Toilers from shops and fields united, The party we of all who work; The earth belongs to us, the people, No room here for the shirk. How many on our flesh have fattened! But if the noisome birds of prey Shall vanish from the sky some morning, The blessed sunlight still will stay.

[Pg 11]

CONTENTS

[Pg 12]

Hitherto, every form of society has been based on the antagonism of oppressing and oppressed classes. But in order to oppress a class, certain conditions must be assured to it under which it can, at least, continue its slavish existence. The serf, in the period of serfdom, raised himself to membership in the commune, just as the petty bourgeois, under the yoke of feudal absolutism, managed to develop into a bourgeois. The modern laborer, on the contrary, instead of rising with the progress of industry, sinks deeper and deeper below the conditions of existence of his own class. He becomes a pauper, and pauperism develops more rapidly than population and wealth. And here it becomes evident that the bourgeoisie is unfit any longer to be the ruling class in society, and to impose its conditions of existence upon society as an over-riding law. It is unfit to rule, because it is incompetent to assure an existence to its slave within his slavery, because it cannot help letting him sink into such a state that it has to feed him, instead of being fed by him. Society can no longer live under this bourgeoisie, in other words, its existence is no longer compatible with society.—Marx and Engels.

[Pg 13]

COMMUNISM AND CHRISTIANISM

ANALYZED AND CONTRASTED FROM THE MARXIAN AND DARWINIAN POINTS OF VIEW

PART I.

Communism: The Naturalistic This-worldly Gospel for the Coming Age of Classless Equality and Economic Freedom—An Open Letter to a Brother Bishop and a Christian Socialist Comrade.

Come over and help us.
Abandon Christian Socialism
for Marxian Communism.

[Pg 14]

FOREWORD [C]

The concept of God, as an explanation of the Universe, is becoming entirely untenable in this age of scientific inquiry. The laws of the persistence of force and the indestructibility of matter, and the unending interplay of cause and effect, make the attempt to trace the origin of things to an anthropomorphic God who had no cause, as futile as is the Oriental cosmology which holds that the world rests on an elephant, and, as an afterthought, that the elephant stands on a tortoise.

The inflexible laws of the known universe cannot logically be held to cease where our immediate experience ends, to make way for an unscientific concept of an uncaused and creating being. The Creation idea is unsupported by evidence, and is in conflict with every scientific law.

Socialism is consistent only with that monistic view which regards all phenomena as expressions of the underlying matter-force reality and as parts of the unity of Nature which interact according to inviolable laws.

Socialism is the application of science, the archenemy of religion, to human social relationships; and just as the basic principle of the philosophy of Socialism finds itself in conflict with religion, so does it, as a propagandist movement, find religion acting against it.

FOOTNOTES:

[C] From the Official Manifesto by the Socialist Party of Great Britain, showing the Antagonism between Socialism and Religion.

[Pg 15]

COMMUNISM: THE NATURALISTIC THIS-WORLDLY GOSPEL FOR THE COMING AGE OF CLASSLESS EQUALITY AND ECONOMIC FREEDOM.

Make the World safe for Industrialism by turning it upside down with Workers above and Owners below.

My dear Brother and Comrade:

Your letter of June 13th [D] relative to the meeting called for the 27th, in the interest of a more radical socialist movement in our church, came duly to hand, and its invitation to attend, or at least write, was highly appreciated.

My days for attending things are, I fear, past. I did not feel able to go to the Annual Convention of the Socialist Party of Ohio, which met much nearer here on the same date, June 27th, and ended on the 29th with a great picnic—a communion, as real and holy, as was ever celebrated. I cannot even be sure of being with you in the House of Bishops during the meeting of the General Convention in October.

However, I intended you to have a letter and set the 26th aside for the writing of it, but I work slowly now and its hours slipped away while I was making notes until only one was left. It was spent in trying to condense all I wanted to say in the letter into a [Pg 16] telegram. What I regard as the best of these efforts was taken to the office at seven p. m. on that day:

Make world safe for democracy by banishing Gods from sky, and capitalists from earth.

Here are four of the many other efforts: (1) Come over and help us. Abandon Christian Socialism for Marxian Communism; (2) Make world safe for democracy by turning it upside down with workers above and owners below; (3) Revolutionize capitalism out of state and orthodoxy out of church; (4) Come over and help us. Abandon reformatory for revolutionary socialism.

What I wanted you to understand is that, in my judgment, there can be no deliverance for the world from the troubles by which it is overwhelmed so long as theism holds the religious field and capitalism the political field.

I.

Religion and politics are the two halves of the sphere in which humanity lives, moves and has its social being. Religion is the ideal and politics the practical half of this sphere. Both halves naturally exist as the result of the same natural law of necessity: the matter-force law which makes it necessary for a man to feed, clothe and shelter his body in order to preserve it and its life.

Marxian socialism is at once this religion and politics, all there is of both of them which is for the good of the world as a whole.

Marxian socialism is a revolutionary movement towards doing away with the existing competitive system for producing and distributing the basic necessities of life (foods, clothes and houses) for the [Pg 17] profit of a few parasites, and substituting a system for making and distributing them for the use of all workers.

So far some competing, lying, robbing, enslaving system for the production and distribution of these necessities has been the basis of every religion and politics—of none more than the Christian and American, and they with the rest have been tried in the balance of experience and found utterly wanting. Indeed, they are making a hell, not a heaven, of the earth in general and of our country in particular.

Christianism as a religion has collapsed. It promised to secure to the world peace and good will, but it has never had more of strife and hate. The tremendous English-German (or if you prefer German-English) war was a conflict at arms between the most outstanding among Christian nations and it was solemnly alleged to have been fought for the high purpose of ending such conflicts; but in reality it scattered the hot coals of war throughout the world, several of which were fanned into blazing by its so-called peace conference and others are ominously smouldering.

Americanism as a politics has collapsed. It promised a classless government of all the people, by all the people, for all the people, but has instead given a government of a class, by a class, for a class. This class, comprising not more than one out of every ten of the population, is the capitalist class, which owns the means and machines for the production of the necessities of life and for their distribution, a class which, as such, though bearing no necessary relationship to either one of the branches of this business, yet realizes enormous profits from both, profits which [Pg 18] are wholly at the expense of the large class, at least nine out of every ten, which does all the work connected with the making of the machines and the operating of them.

This government was to make the country safe for democracy by securing to it the privilege of free speech and free assemblage, the existence of an independent press and the right of appeal for the redress of grievances; but our fathers did not have any too much of these liberties, we have had less and, if the competitive system for the production and distribution of commodities for the profit of the small owning class is to continue, our children are to have none.

Indeed, this is already true of the overwhelming majority, the working class. Its representatives have little if any real part in the government. They are completely subjected to the rule of the owning class. There never has been a body, mind and soul destroying slavery which equaled theirs, either as to the number of men, women and children involved in it, or as to the degrees of misery to which it doomed its victims.

Nor is the end yet. The world war certainly has taken American slavery out of the frying pan into the fire rather than into the water.

American slaves appeal to their government as Jewish slaves appealed to one of their kings for relief and receive the same answer, not in words but in deeds which speak louder:

Thy father made our yoke grievous; now therefore make thou the grievous service of thy father, and his heavy yoke which he put upon us, lighter, and we will serve thee. And he said unto them, Depart yet for three days, then come again to me. And the people [Pg 19] departed. So all the people came the third day as the king had appointed and the king answered them roughly, saying: My father made your yoke heavy, and I will add to your yoke: My father also chastised you with whips, but I will chastise you with scorpions. So when all Israel saw that the king harkened not unto them, the people answered the king, saying, What portion have we in David?

As to details history does not exactly repeat itself and, therefore, I do not believe that the other planets of the universe, of which no doubt there are many billions, are inhabited by human beings of the same type as those of the earth, nor that its men, women and children are to have their bodies reconstructed and resurrected, after they have been disintegrated by death. Such beings on other planets and such reconstructions on this planet would in every case involve a detailed repetition of infinitely numerous processes of evolution which had extended through an eternal past.

Yet in every part of the universe and throughout all eternity, like causes ever have produced and ever shall produce like effect. If, therefore, the course of the Judean masters towards their slaves led to a successful revolt of ten out of twelve tribes, there is every reason for believing that the parallel course which the American masters are pursuing against their slaves will sooner or later issue in a revolution—a revolution which shall do away with both masters and slaves, leaving us with a classless America and a government concerned with the making of provisions for enabling all the people who are able and willing to work to supply themselves in abundance with the necessities of life and with the most [Pg 20] desirable among the luxuries, rather than a government which provides that they who produce nothing shall have the cream and top milk of every necessity and the whole bottle of every luxury, leaving of the necessities only the blue milk for the producers of them and of the luxuries, not even the dregs.

Under this government those who can but will not work will be allowed to starve themselves into a better mind and out of their laziness. The young and the old, the sick and crippled will have their rightful maintenance from the state and out of the best of everything.

The deliverance of the world from commercial imperialism and the making of it safe for industrial democracy would prevent most of its unnecessary suffering and this great salvation is above all else dependent upon a knowledge of the truth. "Ye shall know the truth and the truth shall make you free"—free from all the avoidable ills of life, among them the diabolical trinity of evils, war, poverty and slavery.

The happiness of the world will be promoted in extent and degree in proportion as the knowledge of the truth is disseminated by a twofold revelation: (1) the truth as it is revealed by history according to the Marxian interpretation thereof, a revelation of the truth which is saving the world from the robbing impositions of the capitalistic interpretation of politics, and (2) the truth as it is revealed by nature, according to the Darwinian interpretation thereof, a revelation which is saving the world from the robbing impositions of the supernaturalistic interpretations of religion.

Man has always had as a basis for his thought, belief and action, a system for the production and [Pg 21] distribution of the necessities of life. This is the discovery of Karl Marx which is known as the scientific or materialistic interpretation of history.

According to the scientific interpretation of history which is taught by naturalistic socialism, man is what he is, and his institutions are what they are, because he has fed, clothed and housed himself as he has.

According to the traditional interpretation of history, which is taught by supernaturalistic Christianism, man is what he is because of his thinking, believing and acting with reference to a revelation of a god, as it has been interpreted by his inspired representatives, the great prophets and statesmen, like Isaiah and Luther, Moses and Washington.

Perhaps the best proof of the correctness of the scientific or naturalistic explanation of the career of man and of the incorrectness of the traditional or supernaturalistic one is afforded by the history of morals, the soul of both religion and politics, without which neither could have any existence.

Before the discovery of the art of agriculture, man was dependent for his food upon fruits and nuts, game and fish. When these sources of sustenance failed, the tribes living in the same neighborhood fought with each other in order that the victorious might eat the vanquished.

During this period cannibalism was morally right, and it probably extended through at least two hundred thousand years, even into the Old Testament times. So righteous and holy was it that, in the course of time, the victims were recognized as saviour gods and the drinking of their blood and eating of their flesh constituted a Lord's Supper in which the god was eaten. [Pg 22]

Cannibalism is the basis of our sacrament of the holy communion of bread and wine. As a connecting link between these extremes there was the form of communion which consisted in the eating of animal sacrifices.

By a sacrament with such an origin, you and I render our highest act of worship, though yours is still directed towards one among the supernaturalistic divinities and mine is now directed towards humanity. You say of a divinity: Thou, Lord, hast made me after thine own image and my heart cannot be at rest until I find rest in thee. I say of humanity: Thou, Lord, hast made me after thine own image and my heart cannot be at rest until it find rest in thee.

Within the social realm humanity is my new divinity, and your divinity (my old one) is a symbol of it, or else, so I think, he is at best a fiction and at worst a superstition.

You will be surprised, and I do not expect you to understand me, when I tell you that by translating the services and hymns from the language of my old literalism into that of my new symbolism, I am getting as much good out of them as ever and indeed more. I love the services, especially that great one, the Holy Communion, and the hymns, especially those great ones, Guide Me O Thou Great Jehovah; Lead, Kindly Light; Abide With Me; and Jesus, Lover of My Soul.

My experience has convinced me that the sentimental and poetical elements in religion, to which I attach as much importance as ever, are as readily excited and securely sustained by fixing thought and sympathy upon the martyred human savior, the [Pg 23] working class, as upon a crucified divine saviour, who after all, as the suffering son of God, is but a symbol of the suffering sons and daughters of man, the workers, from whom all good things come.

If grace at dinner means anything, it is addressed to a god who is the symbol of the many workers who did the innumerable things necessary to the producing and serving of it, without whom there would be nothing of all the good things on the table.

In the representation about my pleasure in the services of the church and their value to me, and in many representations scattered throughout this letter, I have in mind the question of an unanswered letter of yours, bearing date, February 25th, 1919, the one in which you ask, in effect, by what right a man can remain in an institution after he has, as I have, abandoned its chief doctrines and aims as they are authoritatively interpreted.

The right of revolution is the one by which I justify my course, and surely no consistent Protestant Christian or American citizen will doubt the solidity of this ground; for Protestantism and Americanism had their origin in revolutions.

Our national declaration of independence contains this famous justification of political revolutions, and it is equally applicable to religious ones, for religion and politics are but the ideal and practical halves of the same social reality:

We hold these truths to be self-evident, that all men are created equal; that they are endowed by their Creator with certain inalienable rights; that among these, are life, liberty, and the pursuit of happiness. That to secure these rights, governments are insti [Pg 24] tuted among men, deriving their just powers from the consent of the governed: that, whenever any form of government becomes destructive of these ends, it is the right of the people to alter or to abolish it, and to institute a new government, laying its foundation on such principles, and organizing its powers in such form, as to them shall seem most likely to effect their safety and happiness. Prudence, indeed, will dictate that governments long established, should not be changed for light and transient causes; and, accord ingly, all experience hath shown, that mankind are more disposed to suffer, while evils are sufferable, than to right themselves by abolishing the forms to which they are accustomed. But, when a long train of abuses and usurpations, pursuing invariably the same object, evinces a design to reduce them under absolute despotism, it is their right—and it is their duty—to throw off such government, and to provide new guards for their security.

Jesus was nothing if he was not a revolutionist. Anyhow, his alleged mother is authoritatively represented as believing him to have been foreordained as one, for this song is put into her mouth:

He hath showed strength with his arm: he hath scattered the proud in the imagination of their hearts.

He hath put down the mighty from their seat: and hath exalted the humble and meek.

He hath filled the hungry with good things: and the rich he hath sent empty away.

This Christian socialism, like Bolshevik socialism, turns the idle rich empty away; but, whereas the Christian gives them no chance to get anything to eat, the Bolshevik allows them to have as much as the poor, if they will work as hard.

Assuming for the sake of argument, that there may have been an historical Jesus who taught some of the [Pg 25] doctrines, in accordance with the representations of the gospel, which are attributed to him, I am nevertheless justified in claiming that he was quite as heretical touching the faith of orthodox Judaism as I am touching that of orthodox Christianism.

As to the Jewish faith he said, in effect, of himself what I say of myself: I have all of the potentialities of my own life within myself. I and my god are one. He dwells in me and I in him, and we are on the earth, not in the sky.

As to the Jewish church and state, Jesus taught that they had become utterly antiquated and that it was the mission of himself and disciples to establish a new heaven, that is to remodel the church; and a new earth, that is, to remodel the state; both remodelings being with reference to the service of humanity by enlightening its darkness and alleviating its misery here and now, rather than teaching it to look for light and happiness elsewhere and elsewhen. [E]

As for the faith and church of orthodox Christianism there is no reason for believing that he would be any more loyal to either than am I. His loyalty was to the truth and to the proletarian, and they (this faith and church) are disloyal to both, being ever on the side of tradition against science, and on the side of the owner against the worker.

Jesus remained in the Jewish church, in spite of his many and great heresies, until he was put out by death. [Pg 26]

My contention is that in view of this example, whether it be, as you think, of an historical or, as I think, of a dramatic character, there is no reason why I should voluntarily go out of the Christian church.

Religion in general and Christianity in particular are nothing unless they are embodiments of morality, and morality does not consist in professions of belief in a god and his revelations as they are recorded in a bible and condensed in a creed, but in a desire and effort to acquire a knowledge of the laws of nature in order that, by conformity to them, life may be made longer and happier.

When this desire exists and this effort is made with reference to one's own self, they constitute morality; when with reference to one's own family and associates, they constitute religion, and when with reference to all others of contemporary and future generations, they constitute Christianity.

But in making such distinctions the fact should not be lost sight of that at bottom there is no difference between morality, religion and Christianity. They are synonyms for the same virtues, the desire and effort to know and live the truth as it is revealed in the doings of nature. There are no other revelations of the truth, nor is there any other morality, religion or Christianity.

Socialism is for me the one comprehensive term which is a synonym at once of morality, religion and Christianity. Marxian and Bolshevikian socialism are two halves of one thing, the theoretical half and the practical half. Marxism is socialism in theory. Bolshevism is (perhaps imperfectly as yet) socialism in practice. [Pg 27]

As long as gods dominate the sky and capitalists prevail upon the earth, the world will be safe for commercial imperialism, having a small heaven for the few rich masters and a large hell for the many poor slaves.

Come over and help us make the world safe for industrial democracy by banishing the personal, conscious gods from the sky and the lying, robbing capitalists from the earth.

But in coming there is no need for leaving your church any more than there is for leaving your state. During the short time which is for me, before the night cometh in which no man can work, I shall remain in both as long as the powers that be allow it, and do what little I can to revolutionize them—revolutionize the church into a school for the teaching of truth instead of lies, and revolutionize the state into a hive for the making of commodities for the use of all instead of for the profit of a few. In doing this I shall be following in the very footsteps of the human Jesus.

After it was discovered that the ground, by planting and cultivating, would produce the necessities of life, when a tribe found that it had too little of it for its growing population, it would go to war with the weaker among adjacent tribes for the purpose of securing its territory; but from this on the vanquished were not eaten, and it was morally wrong to eat them. They were kept alive and put to work at raising harvests for their conquerors, hence arose the institution of slavery, and hence its moral rightness even in this country of the free, down to the beginning of the generation to which I belong.

However, human slavery has never ended, nor will it ever end while the competitive system for the pro [Pg 28] duction of the necessities of life for profit rather than use continues. Human slavery is, so to speak, the basic ingredient of this system.

Speaking broadly, there have been three forms of human slavery—the chattel, feudal and wage slaveries—the third much worse than the first, and the second intermediary between them.

The chattel slave, as the adjective signifies, was the property of his master, as much so as were the horse or the mule with which he worked, and he was cared for in much the same way and for about the same reason.

The feudal slave was as really a chattel as was his predecessor, only he had to look out for himself to a greater extent; and, more was expected from him of accomplishment for the opulence and glory of the master, especially insofar as these depended upon the success of his wars.

The wage slave is, likewise, as really owned by his master as was the chattel or the feudal slave; but, if the master has no need for his service, he is altogether down and out, as the feudal slave was not and still less the chattel, and he has accomplished at least ten times more for his master than did either of his predecessors.

So far man has produced and distributed the necessities of life by a competitive system. The existing form of this competition is known as capitalism. It has supplanted, or at least overshadowed, every other form and is, so to speak, monarch of all it surveys.

The system as it now stands divides the world into two spheres—a small one, in which a few live surfeitingly by owning, and a large one, in which the [Pg 29] many live starvingly by working; and, yet, ultimately, absolutely everything for both depends upon the worker and nothing at all on the owner.

Yes, the worker is indispensable to the owner, as much so as (to use the classical illustration) the dog to the flea; but the owner is no more indispensable to the worker than a flea to a dog. As dogs would be much better off without fleas, so would workers without owners.

The discovery that the itch is caused by a parasite was of an epoch making character because it led to the discovery that many, if not most of the diseases by which mankind and also animal kind are afflicted are of a parasitical character. This is as true of the social organism as of the physical. Capitalism is the tape worm of society.

The existence of the master and slave classes inevitably gives rise to four struggles: (1) the struggle of the slaves with the master for better conditions, issuing in rebellions; (2) the struggle between masters for advantages in markets, issuing in wars; (3) the struggle between the slaves for jobs, issuing in a body and soul destroying poverty; and (4) the struggle of the slaves with the master for a reversal of conditions, issuing in revolutions.

All this struggling between the classes and within them tends towards two results with both classes.

In the case of the master class, these results are the making of the rich fewer and the remaining few richer.

In the case of the slave class, these results are the making of the miserable poor more numerous and all less happy. [Pg 30]

While capitalism stands, all talk about peace on earth and good will among men will be so much hypocrisy; for, until it falls, the world will be divided into the slave and master classes and these four contentions with these results will continue to fill it with hatred and strife.

II.

The overthrow of capitalism in Russia is the greatest event in the history of the world and it has converted International Socialism (the Marxian revolutionary kind) from a theory into a condition.

Theories come and go. Conditions remain and work. From this on revolutionary socialism will be working, night and day, with might and main, here and there, everywhen and everywhere, and its three herculean tasks are: (1) to dethrone the great imperialist, competitive capitalism; (2) to enthrone the great democrat, co-operative industrialism; and (3) to make the world safe for an industrial classless democracy.

In less than three years revolutionary socialism in Russia has accomplished more of these three tasks for the world, than all the states and all the churches with all their wars have done in the whole course of man's career, extending through at least two hundred thousand years. Indeed they never did anything to these ends. On the contrary, what progress has been made towards them was made in spite of their strenuous opposition at every step.

Revolutionary socialism is a world movement towards the deliverance of the producing slave from the non-producing master who has robbed him of the fruits of his toil and left him half dead on the wayside [Pg 31] —the only effective movement to this humanitarian end.

Revolutionary socialism is the Good Samaritan of the despoiled and wounded laborer. The reformatory kinds of socialism are so many priests and Levites who pass by on the other side.

Of no reformatory socialism is this more true than of the Christian kind. Christian socialism is absolutely worthless, and its utter worthlessness is due to the essentially parasitic character of supernaturalistic or orthodox Christianity.

Until the reformation, Christianity was dominated by monks—parasites who lived by begging, lying, and persecuting; and since then by capitalists—parasites who live by robbing, lying and warring.

Monks and capitalists have this in common, that they are natives of the realm of parasitism.

We shall never have peace on earth and good will among men until we have a parasiteless humanity, and we must wait for this until we have a classless world. Parasitism is a boon companion of classism.

Nor can the earth ever be rid of its parasites until the celestial world is rid of the class gods which capitalists have made in their own image and likeness, nor until the terrestrial world is rid of the class states and codes, churches and gospels which their respective class kings or presidents and their class priests or preachers have had the gods of their making impose upon this world, in accordance with their interests and in the furtherance of their lying, robbing, warring schemes for the promotion of them.

Neither capitalism nor Christianism is anything except insofar as it is a system of parasitism and as [Pg 32] parasitic systems they have striking resemblances, nearly as many and close as indistinguishable twins.

Both have gods, churches and priesthoods and these are in each case nothing but symbols.

However, the god of capitalism, though only a symbol, is nevertheless real gold, below a real vault, and nearly all the world sincerely worships it.

But the god of Christianism, though none the less symbolic, but rather more so, is an unreal imaginary spirit, a magnified man without a body, above an imaginary vault, and only a very small part of the world sincerely worships him.

International socialism of the Marxian or Russian type, is for those who starvingly live by working, the most uplifting thing in the world, and for those who surfeitingly live by owning, it is the most depressing thing in the world.

Wise people consider theories without losing too much, if any, sleep on their account, but they study conditions and lie awake nights over them.

Millions of wise Americans have, in the past, been studying socialism as a theory but, in the future, they will study it as a condition, in the only way by which it can rightly and adequately be studied—the way of reading its official documents, accredited periodicals and books. Of all such, the most notable is the Communist Manifesto by Marx and Engels.

This Manifesto is the Marxian gospel. I read two pages in it every day as faithfully as ever I read a chapter in the Jesuine gospel, and with much greater profit; for, whereas the gospel of Marx is exclusively concerned with this terrestrial world, about which I know much and for which I can do a little, the gospel of Jesus is as exclusively concerned with a celestial [Pg 33] world, about which I know nothing and for which I cannot do the least. Here, as a sample of this gospel, I give half of yesterday's reading and most of today's:

The immediate aim of the Communists (Socialists) is the same as that of all the other proletarian parties; formation of the proletariat into a class, overthrow of the bourgeois supremacy, conquest of political power by the proletariat.

The theoretical conclusions of the Communists are in no way based on ideas or principles that have been invented, or discovered, by this or that would-be universal reformer.

They merely express, in general terms, actual relations springing from an existing class struggle, from a historical movement going on under our very eyes. The abolition of existing property relations is not at all a distinctive feature of Communism.

All property relations in the past have continually been subject to historical change consequent upon the change in historical conditions.

The French Revolution, for example, abolished feudal property in favor of bourgeois property.

The distinguishing feature of Communism is not the abolition of property generally, but the abolition of bourgeois property. But modern bourgeois private property is the final and most complete expression of the system of producing and appropriating products, that is based on class antagonism, on the exploitation of the many by the few.

In this sense, the theory of the Communists may be summed up in the single sentence: Abolition of private property.

We Communists have been reproached with the desire of abolishing the right of personally acquiring property as the fruit of a man's own labor, which property is alleged to be the groundwork of all personal freedom, activity and independence.

Hard-won, self-acquired, self-earned property! Do [Pg 34] you mean the property of the petty artisan and of the small peasant, a form of property that preceded the bourgeois form? There is no need to abolish that; the development of industry has, to a great extent, already destroyed it, and is still destroying it daily.

Or do you mean modern bourgeois private property?

But does wage-labor create any property for the laborer? Not a bit. It creates capital, i. e., that kind of property which exploits wage-labor, and which cannot increase except upon condition of getting a new supply of wage-labor for fresh exploitation. Property, in its present form, is based on the antagonism of capital and wage-labor. Let us examine both sides of this antagonism.

To be a capitalist, is to have not only a purely personal, but a social status in production. Capital is a collective product, and only by the united action of many members, nay, in the last resort, only by the united action of all members of society, can it be set in motion.

Capital is therefore not a personal, it is a social power.

When, therefore, capital is converted into common property, into the property of all members of society, personal property is not thereby transformed into social property. It is only the social character of the property that is changed. It loses its class-character.

Let us now take wage-labor:

The average price of wage-labor is the minimum wage, i. e., that quantum of the means of subsistence, which is absolutely requisite to keep the laborer in bare existence, as his labor merely suffices to prolong and reproduce a bare existence. We by no means intend to abolish this personal appropriation of the products of labor, an appropriation that is made for the maintenance and reproduction of human life, and that leaves no surplus wherewith to command the labor of others. All that we want to do away with is the miserable character of this appropriation, under [Pg 35] which the laborer lives merely to increase capital, and is allowed to live only insofar as the interest of the ruling class requires it.

In bourgeois society, living labor is but a means to increase accumulated labor. In Communist society, accumulated labor is but a means to widen, to enrich, to promote the existence of the laborer.

In bourgeois society, therefore, the past dominates the present; in Communist society, the present dominates the past. In bourgeois society capital is independent and has individuality, while the living person is dependent and has no individuality.

And the abolition of this state of things is called by the bourgeois, abolition of individuality and freedom! And rightly so. The abolition of bourgeois individuality, bourgeois independence, and bourgeois freedom is undoubtedly aimed at.

The version of the Marxian gospel which we have in the Manifesto is among the first of its versions. It was published about the middle of the last century. Within the short period which has intervened, it has changed nearly all of the ideas of a large and rapidly growing part of every nation about almost everything social; and before the middle of the present century, it will revolutionize all nations as it has Russia.

Ludendorff, the greatest among the military authorities in Germany, saw and terribly feared this, and called Europe to arms to prevent it. In his almost frantic appeal he said:

Bolshevism is advancing now and in a gradual progress from east to west and is crushing everything between the midland sea and the Atlantic ocean. It was easy to foresee that the Bolshevist armies would attack toward the middle of May and defeat the Poles, as they have now done. The world at large must, [Pg 36] therefore, figure with a Bolshevist advance in Poland toward Berlin and Prague.

Poland's fall will entail the fall of Germany and Czecho-Slovakia. Their neighbors to the north and south will follow. Fate steps along with elementary force. Let no one believe it will come to a stand without enveloping Italy, France and England. Not even the Seven Seas can stop it.

Under the capitalist system most people are and must continue to be slaves. If you are a slave (all wage earners, as such, are slaves) the socialist literature, the greatest of all literatures, will thrill you with the hope of liberty. Read, note and inwardly digest it. No wage earner who does this will ever again vote either the Democratic or the Republican ticket. As a whole this literature is a brilliantly illuminating and almost resistlessly persuasive explanation of the most sane, the most salutary and withal the most promising movement towards the freeing of all toiling men, women and children (nine of every ten) from their body and soul destroying slavery.

Both Socrates and Jesus are recorded as teaching that the saviour of the world is truth. Among saving truths (there is no truth without some saving efficacy) the greatest is the one which was discovered and formulated concurrently by Karl Marx and Frederick Engels and it is in substance this: all which makes for the good of mankind ultimately depends wholly upon the laborious constructors and operators of the machines for the cultivation, production and distribution of the necessities of life, not at all upon the owners of these machines, who at best are idlers and at worst schemers, and in any case parasites.

[Pg 37]

In the beginning was Work. All things were made by it; and without it was not anything made that was made. In it was life; and the life was the light of men.

The opening verses of the gospel according to John have been thus interpreted. The commentator acknowledges that they do not read so now, but contends for good and sufficient reasons, that, if there ever was any truth in them, something to this effect must have been their original reading. Certainly there is no truth in them as they have come down to us.

This representation to the effect that productive labor is the saviour of the world, its real god, the divinity in which we live, move and have our being, is the great truth, the gospel of International Socialism, the greatest of all movements, the movement which carries the only rational hope for the freeing of mankind from all its unnecessary suffering—and the most poignant sufferings, those imposed by the great trinity of evils: (war, poverty and slavery) are not necessary.

Capitalism and Christianism are alike not only in having gods which are symbols, but also in having great buildings set apart for the worshipping of them.

The representatives of the god below the vault worship him in banks under the leadership of a threefold ministry: presidents, cashiers and bookkeepers.

The representatives of the god above the vault worship him in churches under the leadership of a threefold ministry: bishops, priests and deacons.

Speaking particularly of Christianity and America the trouble is not at all with our Brother Jesus and Uncle Sam divinities, but wholly with what they symbolize, capitalism—the god of liars, robbers and warriors. [Pg 38]

What our Brother Jesus and Uncle Sam should alike symbolize are the classless divinities: (1) law, the king of the physical realm, and (2) truth, the queen of the moral realm.

Law is what nature does. There is no other law, and this law is the god of the physical realm. The gods of the supernaturalistic interpretations of religion (Jesus, Jehovah, Allah, Buddha, and all the rest) are personifications, or symbols, of this god, or else they are superstitions.

This representation is proved in practice to be true, on the one hand, by the fact that no one needs to live with reference to any among those gods, not even the god, Jesus; and, on the other hand, by the fact that none who fail to live with reference to this god, law, lives at all.

Every act of nature, that is, every physical and psychical phenomenon which enters into the constitution of the universe, is a word of the revelation of this god, and there is no other revelation. All men must constantly live with reference to it or else immediately die.

Truth is the interpretation of this law in the light of human experience, reason and investigation with the view of making human life, that of self and of all who come or can be brought within the range of one's influence, as long and happy as possible.

Any one who desires and endeavors rightly to learn, interpret and live this law to these ends is moral. In everything is he wholly good and in nothing at all bad.

Religion is not anything good, except only as it is a synonym of such morality, and this is equally true of politics. [Pg 39]

War shortens much life and fills more with misery, hence it is utterly immoral, and this is equally true of poverty and slavery.

In what I say here and in some other places about war being essentially evil, the wars referred to are those by which the world has been cursed through all the ages—wars between different groups of owners with conflicting interests, not the war between owners and workers which is now on. This war will bless, not curse, the world, because it is for the emancipation of the slave class, not for the enrichment of one group of the masters at the expense of another group, at the cost of increased misery to all the slaves on both sides.

If there is any truth in the representation that real religion and real politics alike consist in desiring and endeavoring to make terrestrial life (there is no celestial life of which aught is known) long and happy, the advocate of war is the worst of heretics against Christianism and the worst of traitors against Americanism.

War is a necessary characteristic of vegetables and animals, because they cannot make and operate machines for the supplying of their needs.

Peace is the necessary characteristic of humans, because they can make and operate machines for the supplying of their needs.

Wars between capitalists are inevitabilities, as much so as the wars between two hungry dogs, when one has a bone upon which the lives of both depend. The only difference between capitalists and dogs is, that dogs do their own fighting, whereas capitalists first rob the laborers who produce their commodities, and then persuade or compel them to fight their battles [Pg 40] with fellow capitalists in their competitive efforts to distribute them.

On the one hand it is true that a few capitalists do lose money in wars, and still fewer their lives, but on the other hand it is equally true that the majority of them are made richer and that producing and distributing laborers ultimately bear every cent of the enormous financial burden, and that for every machine owning master who is killed or wounded there are a hundred wage earning slaves.

Yet neither the making nor operating of machines constitutes a man a human. It is co-operation which does this. Nor will co-operation in itself suffice. Bees and ants co-operate and even capitalists do so, yet with all their co-operating bees and ants remain animals and so do capitalists. The co-operation which converts animals into humans is the one which is purposely inaugurated and sustained with the view of securing to each one the fruits of his labor while at the same time increasing them for all—that deliberate co-operation which consists in conscious living, letting live and helping to live.

It is this co-operation which constitutes the most essential difference between the animal and the human. Only animalism can exist and flourish on a competitive basis, yet this is the basis upon which men who falsely claim to be humans are living.

Until mankind begins the construction of a civilization on a foundation of co-operation in the production and distribution of the necessities of life, it should not set up a claim to humanism for itself, because meantime it cannot sustain such a claim.

It is perfectly natural and absolutely necessary for dogs to have belligerent contentions for bones, because [Pg 41] they cannot peacefully co-operate in the making of them; and yet men who can do this are more fierce by far in their competitive struggles for the bones which are necessities to their lives.

Revolutionary socialists of the Marxian or Bolshevikian type offer the only solution of the two great questions of the world at this time: (1) how to save it from its intermittent and lesser hell of suffering by the bloody wars between rival sets of capitalists, and (2) how to save it from its perpetual and greater hell of suffering by the bloodless wars between the machine owning masters and the machine operating slaves, which wars, if less excruciating, are yet more destructive of both life and happiness.

1. As to the bloody wars, a league of nations could prevent them only while the dogs are sleeping off their exhaustion.

Nor could government ownership be depended upon for protection. It would increase the armies and navies, making it next to impossible that more than a decade or two should pass before our children must suffer as much as, or more than, we have by the recent war between the bull dog and the blood hound.

We are not at all indebted to the victory of the bull dog (England) over the blood hound (Germany) for what we have in the way of a guarantee against future wars, but wholly to the presumption of the Newfoundland dog (Russia) which has quietly walked off with the bone of contention while the belligerents were scrapping over it.

Notwithstanding all appearances and impressions to the contrary, this bone never was really Paris or Berlin, but first one and then another country—the Balkan States, Mexico, Persia, Morocco and Russia. [Pg 42]

Of late Russia has been the chief bone of contention. Hence all the snarling against Russian Bolshevism, one of a large litter of puppies born to the Newfoundland since the beginning of the war, representatives of which have already made their way to several countries of Europe, and the prospects are that they or their offspring will soon be in evidence everywhere throughout the world.

When all these Bolsheviki are grown-ups, they will make the world safe for democracy sure enough—not the competitive democracy of the bull dogs and blood hounds, but the co-operative democracy of the Newfoundland dog. Then, and not before, will the world be safe against war.

Since the beginning of the armistice there has been, every now and then, a widespread fear that it might not be permanent, because of a successful effort on the part of the bull dog to put over another war on account of the Russian bone; but for many this fear has now been almost quieted by the total collapse of the Kolchak, Denikin, Yudenich and Wrangel uprisings from within, which were strongly supported by the Allies; and by the repulsion of the Polish invasion which had England, France and the United States behind it.

An astonishing illustration of the truth of the Marxian theory concerning the materialistic or economic determination of history, is furnished by the melancholy fact that the representatives of big business in the allied countries would gladly respond to Gen. Ludendorff's call to join the junkers, against whom they so recently fought, in a war against Russia, of which war Germany would be the battle field. A concerted effort was made to organize such a war, but the wisdom learned in the school of the world war by the [Pg 43] working-men of all the countries to which the call was made and their consequent opposition to the effort caused it to fail.

2. But great as the suffering of the world is on account of the bloody wars of capitalists with each other, it is but a drop in the bucket of sorrow as compared with its suffering on account of the bloodless wars between masters and slaves—between the machine owners and operators. When this bloodless war ceases, as it will with the triumph of international socialism, the bloody wars will cease and not until then.

Under the capitalist system every institution (state, church, school, legislature, court, business, yes, even charity) is necessarily a robbing instrumentality by which a small class of non-producers, fat masters, rob a large class of producers, lean slaves, and rob them twice, each time thrice:

1. The master non-producers rob the slave producers of the three great necessities of physical (body) life—food, clothing and houses.

Even in the United States of America, "the land of plenty," at this time and at all times, seventy-five out of every one hundred are insufficiently fed, clothed and housed.

2. The master non-producers rob the slave producers of the necessities of psychical (soul) life—the liberty to learn the facts of nature, the liberty to humanly interpret and live them and the liberty to teach their discoveries and interpretations.

Even in the United States of America, "the home of political and religious freedom," there is not one who can learn, live and teach the truth without danger of being put out of a synagogue and into a peni [Pg 44] tentiary; and this will continue until imperialistic capitalism and supernaturalistic Christianism, the father and mother of the whole brood of robbers, liars, persecutors and warriors, have been dethroned.

The gods of the capitalistic interpretations of politics and the gods of the supernaturalistic interpretations of religion, symbolize the same reality, parasitic robbery.

Yet within the religious realm the trouble is not with the Jehovahs any more than within the political realm it is with the Sams, but only with what they symbolize.

For one I should feel that both the religious and political realms, which are but halves of the same realm—religion the ideal half, and politics the practical half—would be poorer without their respective Jehovahs and Sams, even as the realm of childhood would be without its Santa Claus.

If symbols are not absolute necessities to the religious and political realms, nevertheless they always have been, now are and probably ever shall be ornaments of them; I hope for their continuance, but as subjectivities, not objectivities.

All the imperialistic interpretations of politics and all the supernaturalistic interpretations of religion must be overthrown, else the world will be lost. The omnipotent, omnipresent saviour who can and will deliver us from them is already in the world. His name is International Communism, the greatest and holiest name which has ever been framed and pronounced; and the gospel of this saviour as it is translated by Thomas Carlyle is written on every wall so that it may be read by all: [Pg 45]

Understand that well, it is the deep commandment, dimmer or clearer, of our whole being, to be freed. Freedom is the one purpose, wisely aimed at, or unwisely, of all man's struggles, toilings, and sufferings, on this earth.

Morality is the greatest thing in the world because without it human life would not be worth the living, or even possible; but, paradoxical as the assertion may seem, freedom or liberty is greater because without it morality would be an impossibility.

One can attain to the very highest standard of morality, religion and sainthood without the least necessity of the slightest reference to what the gods of the supernaturalistic religions said or did, and this is quite as true of Jesus as of any other among such gods, but no man can reach even the lowest standard of morality, and so of course not of religion or sainthood, without constant reference to the god of truth.

Yet there is a difference between a law and a truth. The law is a doing or act of nature, and as such it is a fact or revelation. There are no other facts or revelations.

According to the traditional superstitious conception, a truth is the revelation of the will of a god, involving a service to be rendered directly or indirectly to him, and morality consists in a fulfillment of it.

According to the modern scientific conception, a truth is the interpretation of a fact involving a service to be rendered to men. On the scientific theory each man must have what truth he has, either by his own interpretation or by the adoption for himself of another's interpretation.

No man can live the moral part of his psychical (soul) life on the truth of another any more than he [Pg 46] can live his physical (body) life on the meals of another. Every one must have his own truths, even as he must have his own meals.

Hence the necessity of freedom to morality. Hence, too, the impossibility of the moral life under restraint, such as is imposed by orthodox churches in their official dogmas, and such as is imposed by belligerent states in their espionage laws.

Capitalism is essentially competitive and therefore necessarily belligerent in character: hence a complete, an ideal moral life is an utter impossibility under it, but even the little of moral life which otherwise might be possible is lessened to one-half by official dogmas and espionage laws; if, then, the governments of churches and nations have any regard for the morality of their memberships and citizenships they will at once repeal them, and never enact others.

The democracy which means freedom to learn the laws of the physical realm of nature and to interpret them into laws for the regulation of human life (a democracy which will secure to each one the longest and happiest life which, under the most favorable of conditions, would be within the range of possibilities for him) must wait until the competitive system of capitalism for the production and distribution of the necessities has been universally and completely supplanted by the co-operative system of socialism.

The conclusion of the whole matter, as it is well put by an able contributor to the excellent Proletarian, is this:

What is needed is a complete revolution of the economic system. Private ownership of the tools of wealth production stands in the way of further peaceful social development and private ownership must be [Pg 47] eliminated. The capitalists themselves will not eliminate it. That is certain. It remains for the working class to do so. In order to accomplish this task it will be necessary for the workers to take control of the institution by which the capitalists maintain their ownership of the tools of production—the political state. That is the historic mission of the working class. The mission of the Socialist is to organize and train the workers for this "conquest of political power."

Among the signs of the times which unmistakably point to the great day of the happy consummation of the movement towards the proletarian revolution, and the glorious sky is full of them, is the fact that the world has recently learned from the great war that man must work out his own salvation without the least help from the gods of the supernaturalistic interpretations of religion:

> And that inverted Bowl they call the Sky, Whereunder crawling coop'd we live and die, Lift not your hands to It for help—for It As impotently moves as you or I.
> —Omar.

Yes, and a god moves more impotently than a man; for, whereas the god is driven hither and thither by the laws of matter and force, according to which they co-exist and co-operate through evolutionary processes to the making of the universe what it is, and the god cannot help himself by making it or conditioning himself otherwise, the man, if only he will learn those laws, may combine, guide and ride them to almost any predetermined destination, even out of the class hell of competitive capitalism to the classless heaven of co-operative socialism.

[Pg 48]

III.

The salvation of the world from its unnecessary sufferings is dependent upon such an equitable sharing of the labor involved in the making and operating of the machines of production and distribution, and upon such an equitable sharing of the products as shall issue in a classless mankind by doing away, through a revolution, with the class which lives by owning the means and machines of production and distribution.

It is this advocacy of classless levelism which constitutes the theoretical core of revolutionary socialism. Those who oppose this socialism proceed upon the assumption of the permanency of existing religious and political institutions, the most ruinous of all heresies.

What this heresy is and the fatal policy to which it gives rise has its classic expression, so far as religion is concerned, in the exhortation—"earnestly contend for the faith once for all delivered to the saints"—and, so far as politics is concerned, in the representation—"the laws of the Medes and Persians which altereth not."

There is no such faith in religion, and cannot be, for as a creed becomes stereotyped it loses the religious character and degenerates into superstition.

There are no such laws in politics, and cannot be, for as a law becomes stereotyped it loses the political character and degenerates into tyranny.

Religion, which is the ideal half, and politics, which is the practical half, of the same reality, human socialism, are like all else in the universe, constantly [Pg 49] changing, and necessarily so, because life and progress are dependent upon change.

Orthodoxy in religion and politics is the blight of the ages, because of its assumption that the great institutions, the family, state and church with their customs, laws and doctrines, as they exist for the time being, constitute the foundation of society, without which it could not exist; that these institutions are almost if not altogether what they should be, and that, therefore, the welfare of society, if not indeed its existence, is dependent upon their continuance with but little if any change.

But the foundation of society always has been a system for the production and distribution of the necessities of life, and hence social institutions, customs, laws and creeds are what they are at any time because an economic system is what it is.

If we compare an economic system for the production of the primary necessities of life (foods, clothes and houses) to a king or bishop (we may well do so, for in all ages such systems have been the power behind every regal and episcopal throne) we shall see that states, with their rulers, codes and police, armies and jails; and churches, with their gods, revelations, heavens and hells, are but so many expediencies for the protection of the system from change.

What is true in this respect of the state and church is equally so of the family, the school, the press, the lodge, the club, the library, the theater, the chautauqua and, in short, every institution.

Why all these age-long safeguards against change? Because, so far, every economic system has divided [Pg 50] society into two classes, a comparatively small class who own things and a large one who make things, and if the few honest owners are to hold their own as divinely favored "grab-it-alls," they must be protected at every point against the many dishonest makers who are diabolically tempted to be "keep-somes!"

These rounded out children of god have nothing in common with these caved in imps of the devil, no more than the flea and the dog, or the tapeworm and the man.

David hastily said: All men are liars. He might leisurely have said this of every representative of any religious or political orthodoxy, for they insist that their religion and politics are the permanent elements in social truth which remain unchanged from generation to generation through all ages, whereas no religion or politics continues the same during one decade, nor even a single year.

Orthodox Christians say that Jesus founded their sectarian churches, though each sect insists that he had to do with only one church, theirs. I doubt that he lived. In any case, I am certain that if he did live and founded a church in the first century and were to come to earth again in this twentieth century, he could not if he would and would not if he could become a member of it, because of its changes.

Our own country is different by the width of the whole space of the heavens from what it was before the war, and it is destined to a much wider change.

So far are churches with their doctrines, and states with their laws from being changeless, that they are more or less modified by every development in the [Pg 51] economic system to which they owe their existence and of which they are servants.

In the case of every nation its king, the economic system, has always been a robber and enslaver of the overwhelming majority of the people, and the church and state have been the hands by which he accomplished the robbing and enslaving.

Insofar as they differ, Roman orthodoxy is what it is because of its starting out as the religious product of the feudal system of economics; and Protestant orthodoxy is what it is because of its starting out as the religious product of the capitalistic system of economics.

Protestantism is preferred before Romanism by most of the leading people in the financial world, because it is the child of capitalism, their sister, so to speak, whereas its rival is only a cousin.

As to the Roman and Protestant orthodoxies they are on the same footing. I would not turn my hand over for the difference between them. If literally interpreted in the light of modern science, both are utterly antiquated and irrational.

Orthodox Romanists and Protestants have essentially the same bible and creed. In my opinion, as in that of all Marxian and Darwinian socialists, every supernaturalistic representation in both must be regarded as having either a figurative or a superstitious character, for there is not one among them which can endure a scientific and rational analysis; yet, this is an age of science and reason.

The difference between Romanism and Protestantism is not at all a question of relative supernaturalism, nor of rightness and wrongness, but [Pg 52] wholly one of the difference between the systems of economics which gave them birth.

If you ask, is not this difference at least partly a question of the age in which they took their rise, I reply, yes; but the age itself depends upon the system.

However, it is a fact that while an economic system does constitute the foundation of every religious and political superstructure, yet below the foundation itself there is always a bed rock upon which it ultimately rests, and this is a question of machinery by which the necessities of life are produced and distributed.

The age of feudalism was essentially traditional or theoretical in its character.

The age of capitalism is essentially scientific or experimental in its character.

This difference between these ages is due to the fact that during the earlier age things were made with hand tools, and during the later one with machine tools.

Machinery in a theoretical or traditional age would be an anachronism. It must have an experimental or scientific age for its development, and, paradoxical as it may seem, this the machinery must make for itself. Every period in human history has had its determining character from the tools which brought it into being.

Supernaturalism has no place in the observations, investigations or experimentations which are necessary to the invention, construction and operation of a great machine and, hence, the machines have banished the gods from the roof of the earth and the devils from its cellar, leaving it to us to make of it [Pg 53] what we please, a heaven or a hell without reference to them. In his brilliant work entitled "Social and Philosophical Studies", translated by Charles H. Kerr, Paul Lafargue writes:

> The labour of the mechanical factory puts the wage-worker in touch with terrible natural forces unknown to the peasant, but instead of being mastered by them he controls them. The gigantic mechanism of iron and steel which fills the factory, which makes him move like an automaton, which sometimes clutches him, bruises him, mutilates him, does not engender in him a superstitious terror as the thunder does in the peasant, but leaves him unmoved, for he knows that the limbs of the mechanical monster were fashioned and mounted by his comrades, and that he has but to push a lever to set it in motion or stop it. The machine, in spite of its miraculous power and productiveness, has no mystery for him. The labourer in the electrical works, who has but to turn a crank on a dial to send miles of motive power to tramways, or light the lamps of a city, has but to say, like the God of Genesis, "let there be light," and there is light. Never sorcery more fantastic was imagined, yet for him this sorcery is a simple and natural thing. He would be greatly surprised if one were to come and tell him that a certain god might, if he chose, stop the machines and extinguish the lights when the electricity had been turned on; he would reply that this anarchistic god would be simply a misplaced gearing or a broken wire, and that it would be easy for him to seek and find this disturbing god. The practice of the modern factory teaches scientific determinism to the wage-worker, without it being necessary for him to pass through the theoretic study of the sciences.

Earth must be a hell as long as we allow the capitalist system to continue on it and to enslave the vast majority of its inhabitants. Marxian socialism [Pg 54] will ring out the old era with its hell of human slavery and ring in the new era with its heaven of machine slavery.

One point must be grasped and held by all who would understand the changes which take place within the social realm and it is this: they are due to the differences in the instrumentalities or machines by which the necessities of life are produced.

Man has risen above the lower animals which have common ancestors with his own, because of the superiority of the hand by which he does things to the hands by which they do things. If a man's body in general and hand in particular were not a great improvement over the bodies and hands of the apes, his mind and morality would differ but little from theirs.

The superiority of the civilization of this age over its predecessors is a question of instrumentalities by which the efficiency of the hand is increased.

If all the modern machinery were taken from this generation and replaced by the implements of the stone age the civilization of the next generation would begin to sink, and within a century it would reach the ancient level.

Strong expression is also given to the great truth upon which we are here dwelling by the Socialist Party of Great Britain in its noteworthy Manifesto:

Obviously, in order that there may be ideas and human history, two material things must first be present: human beings, and food and shelter for them. And the fundamental fact that is so seldom realized is, that where, by what means, and how much, food and shelter can be obtained, determines if, where, and how, man shall live, and the forms his social institutions and ideas shall take. [Pg 55]

It is, indeed, the very basis of Socialist philosophy that, in the words of Frederick Engels:

"In every historical epoch the prevailing mode of economic production and exchange, and the social organization necessarily following from it, form the basis upon which is built up, and from which, alone can be explained, the political and intellectual history of that epoch."

This materialist concept is the Socialist key to history. It is the first principle of a science of society, and, being directly antagonistic to all religious philosophy, it is destined to drive this "philosophy" and all its superstitions from their last ditch.

Civilization will not die with the death of the capitalist system of production any more than it did with the feudal system. It improved under capitalism, because of the improvement in the machinery of production, and it is destined to continue its progress so long as new and better machines are made and this will be to the end.

Marxian socialism is a machine optimism. Under this socialism the number and efficiency of machines would increase more rapidly than they have under capitalism and feudalism, because its aim will be the production of commodities for use within the shortest time by the least exertion at the slightest risk of injury.

Up to the point of over production, that is, of glutting the markets, it is to the interest of capitalism to encourage improvements in machinery, but the ability to do this has been reached, as is evident from what we hear at increasingly frequent intervals about an over production of commodities.

What machinery we now have renders it possible to produce more commodities than can be sold with [Pg 56] out employing all the labor power. But the idle, starving slave is a danger to the idle, surfeiting master. Hence, under capitalism there can be no further development of machinery, at least not on a large scale.

An industrial government would have for its aim to produce enough of everything for all with the least expenditure of energy and time. Hence, the greatest benefactors and heroes under socialism would be the inventors of labor saving, leisure giving machinery.

We hear much about the mental superiority of the representatives of the master class over those of the slave class, but there is little or no truth in it.

On the contrary, it can be shown that the invention of a great labor saving, rapid-producing machine is, upon the whole, the greatest triumph of the human mind and that nearly all among such machines are invented, made, operated, kept in order and improved by the laborer.

Masters may be more cunning than slaves, but cunningness is not an evidence of a high order of intellectual power. Many of the lower animals are quite the equals, if not indeed the superiors, of capitalists in this quality, but no animal is the equal of any man, not to speak of the exceptionally skilled laborer, in the power to produce efficient machines for the production and distribution of the necessities of life.

Romanism began its career as a child of the feudal system for the production and distribution of commodities for the profit of the owners of the land and the means for its cultivation. The mission to which it was born was the assistance of its father, feudalism, in robbing and enslaving the workers who tilled the [Pg 57] soil, and never did a servant more faithfully or efficiently perform a task during a longer period.

Protestantism began its career as a child of the capitalistic system for the production and distribution of commodities for the profit of the owners of the means and machines for their manufacturing. The mission to which it was born was the assistance of its father, capitalism, in robbing and enslaving the workers, who make and operate the machines, and never did a servant more faithfully and efficiently perform a task in a larger or more fruitful field.

Hitherto all systems of economics have had the same soul, competition; and, because of it, every one among them has been a diabolical trinity of which lying is the father; robbing is the son, who proceeds from the father; and murder is the spirit, who proceeds from the father and the son.

Labor, "the certain man" of every nation, is half dead lying in the ditch by the wayside, despoiled and wounded, the victim of capitalism, the greatest liar, robber and murderer of all the ages.

The church is the archangel or prime minister through which this Beelzebub, capitalism, has done most of his lying, though within the last hundred years the business has become so great that the office of coadjutor to this archangel was created, and the press appointed to it.

The state is the archangel or prime minister through which this prince of devils, capitalism, has done most of his robbing and killing, though the church has often taken a helpful hand in these departments of the devil's work, the great work of converting earth into a hell. [Pg 58]

Nearly all of the backwardness of the world and more than half of its unnecessary sufferings have been due to efforts to prevent changes in religion and politics. Our nation is passing through the darkest period of its history because of such efforts on the part of the powers which be in the state, and they are supported by those in the church.

Speaking of the change with which we are here especially concerned, the one involved in the supplanting of an old economic system by a new, there have been several revolutions due to such changes, and another is inevitable and imminent.

When an economic system fails, as the capitalistic one is failing, to feed, clothe and house the workers of the world who produce all foods, clothes and houses, the time when it must give place to another is manifestly near at hand.

Capitalism is failing in this, the only legitimate mission of an economic system. It has indeed over-supplied the needs of about one in ten, but in doing this it has shown partiality, for the remaining nine are left more or less foodless, clotheless and houseless, and this notwithstanding they have done all the feeding, clothing and housing. Those favored by the system will not be able to prevent its overthrow by those who are wronged.

With our materials, factories, railroads and skill, all should have enough and to spare of every necessity, but so far is this from being the case that millions are insufficiently fed, clothed, housed and warmed, and are doomed to a perpetual and exhaustive drudgery which leaves neither leisure nor energy for the cultivation of their soul life. [Pg 59]

The economical and statistical experts of our government's Department of Labor represent that the bare necessities of a comfortable and efficient life for a family of five require an annual income of $1,500, and that the simple luxuries, which are next to being indispensable, require an additional $1,000, in all $2,500, per year.

How many American families of five have even the smaller of these sums at their disposal? The overwhelming majority have less than $1,000. Let us be honest with the peoples of other nations by ceasing to speak of our country as "the land of plenty and the home of the free," until there is a great change for the better.

Wage slavery may be prolonged by a military coercion but it cannot have a successor in any other form of human slavery. Military coercion prolonged chattel slavery, and by so doing brought what is known as the dark ages upon the world. If wage slavery is to be prolonged by military coercion the world must pass through a second dark age. The league of nations is fixing for this; but let us hope that this coalition will not stand and that wage slavery will soon be followed by machine slavery, the form of slavery which will end human slavery; not until then shall we have peace on earth and good will among men.

Then they shall beat their swords into plowshares, and their spears into pruning hooks: nation shall not lift up sword against nation, neither shall they learn war any more.

Do you not now see with me that the christ of the world is not a conscious, personal god, but an un [Pg 60] conscious, impersonal machine? It is the machine of man, not a lamb of god, to which we may hopefully look for the taking away of the sins of the world.

Ignorance is the great misfortune of the world, its devil, and slavery is his hell. The machine is the redeemer who shall save man from this devil and hell.

Yes, strange, even blasphemous, as the representation may seem, it is nevertheless true, the machine is the only name given under heaven whereby the world can be saved.

Civilization is salvation. The civilization which is salvation depends on leisure and it on slavery, but so long as leisure is dependent upon the slavery of man, civilization must be limited to a diminishing few.

Marxian socialism is a movement towards the equalization and universalization of leisure by doing away with the master and slave classes, through transference of slavery from man to machine.

If there is any truth in my naturalistic representation about the dependence of morality upon a system for the production of the necessities of life, there is none in the supernaturalistic one, which makes it dependent on any among the gods; and, what is true of the realm of morality is equally so of the realm of history, and this whether it be the history of the universe in general or man in particular.

Lavoisier and Mayer showed that no god (Jesus, Jehovah, Allah, Buddha) created the universe out of nothing, for the matter and force which enter into its constitution are eternalities and universalities. [Pg 61]

Kant and Laplace showed that the earth and the heavenly bodies were not created by any god at all, but evolved from gaseous nebulae.

Kepler and Newton showed that these bodies were not governed in their motions by a god but by the law of gravitation.

Darwin and Wallace showed that the species of animal and vegetable life were not created by any among the gods, but evolved from a common protoplasm.

Marx and Engels showed that man's career has not been determined by any among the gods, but by his systems for producing and distributing the necessities of life.

These ten men are the greatest teachers the world has had, and this is the sum of all their great teachings: The universe is self-existing, self-sustaining and self-governing, having all the potentialities of its own life within itself, and what is true of it in general is equally so of all the phenomena which enter into its constitution, including man; who, though he is the highest among them, is only a phenomenon, on a level with all the rest, not excepting the lowest. A microbe and a man are on the same footing, both as to their origin and destiny, and as to their having within themselves all power which is available for making the most of their respective lives.

> "We are part Of every rock and bird and beast and hill, One with the things that prey on us, And one with what we kill."

Darwinism and Marxism constitute one gospel, the only true, comprehensive and sufficient gospel which [Pg 62] the world has ever had or can have, and there is no hope for the future of mankind except in it. If it fails the world is lost, but it shall not and indeed cannot fail, for its words are so many acts or facts of nature.

There is no fact which is not such an act, and every such fact is a part of the one only law upon the knowing and doing of which terrestrial life and its happiness are wholly and solely dependent.

Yes, life, long life, happy life, all there is of such human life, or divine life, (if there be any), depends entirely upon a knowledge of and conformity to this law which is the doing of nature, and not at all upon any law which is the willing of a god, if indeed there is such a law.

Neither the religion nor the politics which enters into the constitution of Marxian or proletarian socialism is at all concerned about the heaven above or the hell below the earth, if there are such places: but the concern of both is wholly to ring out a hell from the earth and to ring in a heaven upon it.

Nor have the religion and politics which constitute this socialism the least concern about the service of a celestial divinity (Jesus, Jehovah, Allah, Buddha or any other) by doing his will; but both are much concerned with the service of humanity, which consists in rightly learning, interpreting and using the laws of nature, wholly for the purpose of making the terrestrial lives of men, women and children as long and happy as possible, and with absolutely no reference to any celestial life which may be either above or below the earth.

Religion and politics are the complementary and [Pg 63] inseparable halves of the social sphere, religion being its idealism and politics its practicalism.

Religious idealism is a social soul of which the church should be the embodiment.

Political practicalism is a social soul of which the state should be the embodiment.

Contrary to the representations of orthodox Christianism it is impossible for any soul to exist without an embodiment.

In truth the body produces the soul, not the soul the body. We must have the church and state in order that we may have their souls, idealism and practicalism.

Why, if the Soul can fling the Dust aside And naked on the Air of Heaven ride, Were't not a Shame—were't not a Shame for him In this clay carcass crippled to abide?
—Omar.

IV.

The church and the state are on the same level as to their origin and importance. Both are human institutions and each is indispensable to the other. It is not at all desirable or possible to rid the world of either, but it is absolutely necessary that both should be revolutionized, the church by having its bible and creed rewritten or at least reinterpreted, on the basis of truth as it is revealed by nature, and the state by having its institutions reorganized on the basis of service to all instead of only to those of a small class, the owner or master class.

All the idealistic aims of churches and all the practical undertakings of states should be directly concerned with the answer to three questions: (1) [Pg 64] the question as to how to reach the goal where terrestrial life shall in the case of each man, woman and child be as long and happy as it is within the range of possibilities to make it, by the fullest of attainable knowledge concerning the laws of nature; (2) the question as to how to make the most successful endeavor universally to disseminate such knowledge, and (3) the question as to how resistlessly to persuade to the living of it.

These are the only concerns and aims of Marxian socialism and they cannot be promoted or even avowed by Christian socialists.

The great crime of the ages is the robbing of the producer of the basic necessities of human life by the non-producer.

Capitalism is the robber, and the politics and religion of the old states and churches are the right and left hands by which he has been and is doing the robbing.

Marxian socialism is an undertaking which has for its task the overthrow of the system which makes it possible for those who produce nothing to live surfeitingly, and renders it necessary for those who produce everything to live starvingly.

Poverty is a disease caused by the unjust wage system of competitive capitalism for producing and distributing the necessities of life (food, clothing and shelter) for the profit of capitalists, the few who live by owning the materials and machines of production and distribution; and this blighting malady cannot be cured by charity, but it will spread until this system is supplanted by the just one of co-operative industrialism, a system by which these necessities shall [Pg 65] be produced and distributed for the use of laborers, those who live by making and operating the machines.

Every gift to charity by a rich man is a robbery of a poor man. You will not see this at once, if ever, and I shall not blame you for the failure to do so. It was not seen by me until I was much older than you; but I am now seeing it as clearly as I ever saw the sun on a cloudless noonday, and this is true of rapidly growing millions who are resolutely resolved to do away with the prevailing conception of charity, according to which capitalists may rob laborers of the fruit of their toil, giving them of it barely enough to keep body and soul together and to raise up children who are doomed to follow in their footsteps; and then, when the strength of their victim fails, to make amends for the robberies, by giving the most highly favored among them beds in hospitals, poor-houses in which to die prematurely, and nameless graves in potter's fields in which to await hopefully a resurrection and ascension to an inheritance of happiness in a sky, which was denied them on the earth.

The time is at hand when everywhere the unemployed and the underpaid shall begin a resistless march towards the goal of economic levelism under a banner containing this slogan: We want no charity but the right to work and the fruits of our labors that we and our helpless dependents may have every necessity to the fullest life for body and soul.

During more than a whole generation Mrs. Brown and I have not produced a spoonful of any food, a thread of any garment or a shingle of any house; and yet we have had foods, garments and houses in abundance with some to spare, while their [Pg 66] producers have had them in scarcity with much to want.

While the world war was on, an ill wind for the producers blew a thousand dollars to us and an ill wind for us blew it into the hands of a committee, ostensibly for investment on behalf of a hospital of which we approved, but really for the purchase of a bond in the interest of a war of which we disapproved.

The fathers of the present generation of producers and distributors of the necessities of life were robbed in order that we might inherit the property from which our income is derived; the sons and daughters are being robbed over and over again and again, year after year, in order that the property may continue to yield this income to us.

We therefore paid nothing of our own for this bond. What we gave for it was of the spoils which the great robber, capitalism, has bestowed upon us, its favorite children, from what it has taken from its unfortunate victims.

The same persons or their children and successors were or shall be robbed first to create our property, then to pay the income of it, next to buy the bond, and now they are being robbed to meet the interest on it and finally they will be robbed to pay its face value. If capitalism stands, of course the victims of the last of these robberies will belong, probably, to a remote generation; but this delay is a misfortune in store for many of all intervening generations.

If the robbery connected with this bond were limited to its original cost, one thousand dollars, and to its accruing interest, which is likely in time to ag [Pg 67] gregate several thousand dollars, it would indeed be bad enough, yet not nearly as much so as it is under the melancholy circumstances; for the money paid on account of the bond goes towards killing or wrecking its producers, if not those who produced this particular thousand dollars, yet others of their class to whom the world owes all of its wealth; therefore the thousand dollars which went into this bond has been devoted to the robbery of those who were robbed of it and of the most precious of all things: life and limb.

You will ask: how can you and Mrs Brown, in the face of your theory, according to which all who live by owning are robbers of those who live by working, consistently receive and expend the income of your inheritance?

The answer was given to a friend who asked us why we did not follow the heroic example of a young American who had recently renounced what had been inherited by him, and this is, in effect, what we said:

As we look at the question, our course is more rational than his, because the wealth which he renounces may go to some one who is without his sympathy for the proletariat. We prefer to receive our inheritance and use it to overthrow the economic system which makes it possible for us to do nothing and have everything, and for those who do everything to have nothing.

Capitalists, as such, people who live by the owning of the machines of production and distribution, instead of by the making and operating of them, have much to say against the alleged anarchism of socialists and yet they are necessarily what they accuse anarchism of being, robbers and murderers. [Pg 68] Every cent of profit, interest and rent is so much robbing, and all wars are so many conflicts between the capitalistic bandits or robbers in the countries involved, and the peace conferences, which follow them, are so many attempts of the bandits on the successful side to have the spoils as large as possible, and to satisfactorily divide them.

It is Holy Week 1921. The week in which during all the years of many and long ages benighted people sacrificed their Christs to Shylock gods. If Jesus lived and was a Christ, unhappily He was neither the first nor the last, for there were many both before and after Him. Were they who superstitiously led these victims to their Golgothas greater sinners against humanity than those who did avariciously during the war drive large armies of young men to the terrible trenches, a wholesale sacrifice of the lords of power and wealth and who do now drive the vast majority of the nations involved in that war to a terrible body and soul destroying poverty and slavery? No. The modern robbers even more than the ancient ones are in need of the prayer: Forgive them for they know not what they do.

Communism and Christianism have, indeed, this in common, that their object is to promote life, long life, and happy life, both lives in a large and full measure, pressed down, shaken together and running over.

Yet, with this sameness in the gospels of Communism and Christianism there is this difference in the aims of the christs who preached them, which separate them as widely as the east is from the west, leaving a great and impassable gulf between them.

Marx, the christ of the Communist gospel, said: I am [Pg 69] come that the world might have terrestrial life for body, mind and soul, and have it for each in the fullest of possible measures by co-operation with each other in the discovery of the laws of nature and in making them serve men, women and children by securing for them food, clothing, shelter, health and comfort for the body, and leisure for the mind to think and for the soul to grow.

Jesus, the christ of the Christian gospel, according to orthodoxy, said: I am come that ye might have celestial life for mind, body and soul and have it for each in the largest and fullest possible measure by co-operation in persuading each other in particular and the world in general to receive a revelation of the will of a conscious, personal God, made through prophets, preserved in the bible and interpreted by the church.

With me it is a melancholy but resistless and deepening conviction, that, if orthodox Christianism should become associated with Marxian socialism, as Kingsley and you would associate them, we should soon have a glaring illustration of the truth of two proverbs: a house divided against itself cannot stand; and no man can serve two masters.

Moreover, I believe that if Christian socialism were to become a door to Marxian socialism, through which orthodox Christianism could enter and make itself at home, the revolutionary aims of the slave class would be thwarted and the world would enter upon a new dark age, as it did when Constantine was converted to Christianity and Christians became the most loyal citizens and valiant soldiers of the Empire.

At that time chattel slavery had run its course as [Pg 70] wage slavery has now; and, if it had not been prolonged by a military despotism, as I fear this may be, the world would have had something of the feudal slavery, but nothing of the dark age. This age was the baneful fruit of Christianism. Christianity has held the world back from civilization instead of advancing it towards civilization.

The Christianization of Marxian communism, in accordance with the program of Kingsley and our Church Socialist League, would spell another military despotism for the prolongation of a second system of slavery, which has run its course and is in a fair way of being overthrown; but if the revolutionists fail, as the result of being trampled under the iron heel, we are at the threshold of a second dark age and shall soon be passing through all the miseries of it.

My interest in the movement within our church looking towards a Christian socialism of a more radical and revolutionary type would be great, if only I could feel as I should so much like, that the Christian socialism to which you have consecrated the whole prime of your life, and the Marxian socialism, to which I have consecrated all of the little that remains of mine, the fag-end, are not utter incompatibilities, so much so that it is absolutely impossible that they can co-exist and co-operate to any good purpose.

The irreconcilable incompatibility of Christian socialism and Marxian socialism is due to the fact that, whereas the Christian is essentially imperialistic in its character, the Marxian is as essentially democratic. The reason for this fundamental and ineradicable difference, and the consequent incompatibleness, is the fact [Pg 71] that orthodoxism, whether Christian, Jewish, Mohammedan or Buddhistic, is nothing unless it is supernaturalistic and traditional; and Marxism is nothing unless it is naturalistic and scientific, as much so as is Darwinism.

In order that you may see the reason, as I understand it, for this wide, deep and bridgeless difference, I draw the following contrasts between the essential beliefs of Marxian socialists and orthodox Christians:

1. Marxian socialism is essentially naturalistic. Orthodox Christianism is essentially supernaturalistic. The consistent socialist says: I have all the potentialities of my own life within myself. The consistent Christian says: My strength is from God.

2. Marxian socialism is essentially classless. Orthodox Christianism is essentially a class system by which the world is divided into

two classes, saints and sinners. The consistent socialist says: Every man is my brother. The consistent Christian (like the theist of every name—Jew, Mohammedan, Buddhist and the rest) says: Every true believer is my brother, but those who are not are only potential brethren.

3. Marxian socialism is essentially terrestrial. Orthodox Christianism is essentially celestial. The consistent socialist says: Earth is my home. The consistent Christian says: Heaven is my home.

4. Marxian socialism is essentially materialistic. Orthodox Christianism is essentially spiritualistic. The consistent socialist says: The basic necessities of life, and therefore its first concern, are foods, raiments, shelters, comfort and leisure. The consistent Christian says: Take no primary thought for these, but only for faith in and obedience to God, regarding all else of secondary importance. [Pg 72]

5. Marxian socialism is essentially proletarian. Orthodox Christianism is essentially bourgeois. The consistent socialist says: I am, by reason of my antecedents, a man, a woman, a child of nature on an essential level as to my origin and destiny with every other representative of humanity and indeed animality. The consistent Christian, like the theist of every name, says: I am (by reason of my faith, baptism or conversion) a prince or princess, the son or daughter of a king, God.

6. Marxian socialism is essentially democratic. Orthodox Christianism is essentially imperialistic. The consistent socialist says: I live with reference to the will of the majority. The consistent Christian says: I live with reference to the will of a God.

7. Marxian socialism is essentially pacific. [F] Orthodox Christianism is essentially belligerent. The consistent socialist says: Since you are a man, I [Pg 73] co-operate with you. The consistent Christian says: Since you are not a believer, I contend with you.

8. Marxian socialism is essentially non-sectarian. The consistent socialist says: All the world is my home and the desire and effort to render service to men, women and children is my religion. The consistent Christian says: Only Christendom is my home and the desire and effort to serve a God is my religion.

9. Marxian socialism is, as to the source of knowledge and the means of attaining it, essentially scientific. Orthodox Christianism is essentially traditional. The consistent socialist says: The salvation of the world is dependent upon what is learned by natural experience, observation and investigation about the doings of a matter-force-law, nature. The consistent Christian says: This salvation depends upon what is learned by revelation, tradition and inspiration about the willings of a father-son-spirit, God.

10. Marxian socialism explains the history of mankind on the naturalistic theory that it has been determined during every period by the existing system for supplying the materialistic necessities of life. Orthodox Christianism explains this history on the supernaturalistic theory that it is determined by the providential directions of a triune divinity. The consistent socialist says: If you will tell me of the economic system by which a people have fed, clothed and housed themselves, I will tell you, at least in general outline, what has been their history. The consistent Christian says: If you will tell me what the providences of my God have been towards a people, I will tell you their history.

11. Marxian socialism has inscribed on one of its [Pg 74] banners: Liberty. Orthodox Christianism has this inscription on its corresponding banner: Obedience. The consistent socialist says: This Liberty-banner is the symbol of my freedom as a son of man to be progressively learning, living and teaching the unfolding revelations of nature—to know and to live which is to have life, terrestrial life in an ever increasing measure, all the life there is here and now or elsewhere and elsewhen, if there is to be a conscious, personal life anywhere or anywhen else. The consistent Christian says: This Obedience-banner is a symbol of my slavery as a son of God by which I am bound to receive, live and teach the faith once for all delivered to the saints in the Old and New Testaments or else lose the permanent life in the sky which is to follow this temporary one on the earth.

12. Marxian socialism has inscribed on another of its banners: Justice to Man. Orthodox Christianism has on its corresponding banner: Love to God. The consistent socialist says: It is my aim to do unto others as I would have them do unto me if our circumstances

were reversed. The consistent Christian says: It is my aim to love God with all my heart, mind and soul.

And if there be any further contrast between this Christianism and Socialism, it is briefly comprehended in these three statements,—in themselves sufficient to show how absolutely impossible it is for a consistent Jesuine Christian to be a consistent Marxian Socialist:

1. Marx seeks to save by doing away with both the master and slave classes—Jesus by exalting the slave class above the master class.

2. Marx exhorts the slave class to look to itself [Pg 75] for deliverance—Jesus taught it to look to a God for this.

3. Marx promises salvation for this world here and now, a world about which everybody knows much—Jesus promised it for another world elsewhere and elsewhen, a world about which nobody knows anything.

The world has never had a gospel which is at all comparable in its excellency to that of Marxian Socialism. The gospel of Jesuine Christianism, according to the orthodox interpretation of it, is no exception; for, granting it to be superior to the Mosaic, Buddhistic, Mohammedan and other gospels, it is, nevertheless, almost infinitely inferior to the Marxian gospel. Gospels are for the purpose of saving the world from its suffering. The Jesuine and Marxian gospels are alike in having for their object the salvation of the proletarian world.

V.

About three years ago I discovered that I had spent a long, strenuous and open-handed ministry in preaching lies to the permanent ruin of my health and the temporary embarrassment of my purse; therefore I had the unhappy experience of being forced to see that all this part of my life, its prime, had been mostly, if not wholly wasted and worse. What was to be done?

My friends told me as plainly as they could, and some succeeded in making it brutally plain, that in losing my faith in the supernaturalistic dogmas of traditional Christianism, as they are literally in

[Pg 76] terpreted in the doctrinal standards of the orthodox churches, I had lost the pearl of great price.

My soul told me that I had never possessed this jewel, but that, even with the little time and enfeebled strength that remained to me, I might yet find it, if only I should cease looking for it in the field of supernaturalism, under the direction of divine authority, and begin looking for it in the field of naturalism, under the direction of human reason.

Happily, where faith went out courage came in, and it increased with my desperation until (though standing on the shore of death where the deep and unknown stream lies darkly between the present and future) I could and I did undertake the supreme task of my life—the breaking of the chains by which I was bound as a slave to the degrading superstition that I was, both by an inherited and cultivated disposition, a doomed man, and by an inherent weakness, a helpless one with no power to emancipate myself.

Of such enslaving chains I mention three among the strongest, the severed parts of which, with those of all the rest, now lie scattered about me: (1) the chain of the fear of God; (2) the chain of the fear of the devil, and (3) the chain of the fear of man.

Hitherto I had been a child, thinking as a child, understanding as a child and speaking as a child.

Henceforth I was to be a man, the greatest, conscious, personal being who has anything to do with this world; and as a man, I put away the things of a child, especially the most childish of all things, fear, the fear of God, the fear of devil and the fear of man.

Preachers of the supernaturalistic interpretations [Pg 77] of religion say that the fear of God is salvation. It is damnation. No one who has fear of any conscious, personal master whomsoever or wheresoever, God in heaven, devil in hell or man on earth, is free or other than a slave. Nor has any such attained to the full stature of manhood.

There is only one fear which saves and that is the fear of ignorance. The world's destroyer-god is ignorance. There is no other devil on earth or in hell below it, and this one lives, moves and has his being in the fear of knowledge.

The world's saviour-god is knowledge. There is no other Christ on earth or in any heaven above it, and this one lives, moves and has his being in the fear of ignorance.

Happily, I listened to my soul and I have found the pearl of great price, yes, a whole bed of them, so that I am now in position to substitute in my preaching a truth for every lie I used to preach, and thus save myself; but woe unto me unless I make the substitution by ringing out the lie and ringing in the truth.

Within the last three years I have learned that, as I have not been, since the beginning of my Christian ministry, more than a generation ago, a producer, I have nothing of my own to give to charity, and what is true of me is true of Mrs. Brown.

No one is a producer who does not grow things on the farm, make things in a shop, discover things in a laboratory or render some necessary or helpful service to those who do such things. I have done nothing of the kind. If I had been preaching truths [Pg 78] I might have rendered such service, but I preached lies.

Every possession rightfully belongs to the productive worker and nothing to the unproductive idler. This is one of the two greatest and most salutary among all the truths known to mankind. Recently I made acknowledgment of it on the pledges to a good cause, that of the Red Cross, by writing on their upper left hand corners: "The gift of Unknown Laborers through Bishop and Mrs. Brown, whose possessions are the fruits of their enforced toil and sacrifices."

By this acknowledgment I rang out a great lie—the lie which makes the salvation of the world depend upon the capitalists with their servants, the preachers on the right and the politicians on the left hand.

Salvation or, what is the same reality, civilization, always has been and always will be dependent upon the producer. It will never be attained until the laboring class has done away with the capitalist class. The ideal civilization (which is the salvation of the world from its unnecessary sufferings, especially the overwhelming ones due to the great trinity of evils, war, poverty and slavery) is in the very nature of things an impossibility on the basis of class sectarianism, such as we have even in our Anglo-American Christianity, the best interpretation of traditional religion, and in our American democracy, the best interpretation of traditional politics.

Among the pathetic things about war, there is this, the laboring class makes by far the greater sacrifices, not only of life and limb, but also of money. [Pg 79]

Quite contrary to the general impression, capitalists, as such, pay no part of the enormous and ruinous pecuniary cost of war. When Mr. Rockefeller pays out three million dollars in war taxes he is disposing of what rightfully belongs to laborers, because they, not he, earned it. Capitalists, as such, neither earn nor pay anything, in time of either war or peace.

So much for one of the two great truths. The other, which is the greater because it includes its companion, is this: Man has within himself all the potentialities of his own life. This is true of the universe as a whole, and, therefore, necessarily so of all that therein is.

The sum of both truths is that the salvation of the world is wholly dependent upon productive laborers and that they must look individually only to the exertion of their own mental and physical powers and collectively to co-operation with each other for the accomplishment of their mission.

Through the whole of my past ministry in the field I rang out these great truths and rang a great lie in by representing that the salvation of the world depends upon a potentiality which is in the sky and not in man, that heaven is above the earth and hell below it, not on it.

When I commenced my present ministry in the study,

> I sent my Soul through the Invisible, Some letter of that After-life to spell; And by and by my Soul return'd to me, And answer'd 'I Myself am Heaven and Hell!'

Omar, the poetic astronomer, might have added a stanza which would have closed. "I myself am God." [Pg 80] This is, in effect, what Jesus did say: "I and my Father are one." This is as true of you and me and of every man, woman and child as it was of Jesus.

And Jesus represented that God, both as Father and Son, dwells in the hearts of believers. But every relevant fact which has been scientifically established as such (and there is a whole mountain of such facts) points to the conclusion that Christians are no more divine than other people, and that, as to his essential nature, no man would be less divine than he is if Jesus had never been born.

Gods in the skies (Jesus, Jehovah, Allah, Buddha) are all right as subjective symbols of human potentialities and attributes and of natural laws, even as the Stars and Stripes on a pole, Uncle Sam in the capitol and Santa Claus in a sleigh are all right as such symbols; but such gods are all wrong, if regarded as objective realities existing independently of those who created them as divinities and placed them in celestial habitations.

What is true of the gods is equally so of all the supernaturalistic dogmas of the several traditional interpretations of religion. Insofar as they are not pure superstitions they are symbols of imaginary events which people think should or must have occurred in the past or should or must occur in the future; not statements of historical events which have occurred or are to occur.

So far I have not found it necessary to renounce the Christian God or any of the things which go with him and I have no idea of doing this, any more than I have of renouncing the American Uncle Sam and the things which go with him, but I place the Brother [Pg 81] Jesus of the Christian religion and the Uncle Sam of the American politics on the same footing with each other and with others of their kind as subjective realities. I could be a Jew and an Englishman as conscientiously as a Christian and an American. Many of the early Christians were also Pagans, worshippers of other Gods than Jesus.

Nor is this all or even much more than half of my religious and political levelism.

On the one hand as a religionist I can be any and everything but an orthodox sectarian. This orthodoxy is a libel against humanity. The world owes to it a great part of all its unnecessary troubles—those which are brought about by the triune devil of persecution, ignorance and superstition.

On the other hand as a politician I can be any and everything but a nationalistic sectarian. This nationalism is a libel against humanity. The world owes to it a great part of all its unnecessary troubles—those which are brought upon it by the triune devil of war, poverty and slavery.

Hoping that you will abandon Jesuine socialism for Marxian communism and join me in an effort to banish the fictitious, superstitious gods from the skies and the lying, robbing capitalists from the earth, I am with every good wish,

Very cordially yours,
WM. M. BROWN.

Brownella Cottage,
Galion, Ohio.

FOOTNOTES:

[D] This letter was written in July, 1919, and sent to the press in September, 1920. In the interim several of its representations and arguments were made more complete: therefore, some among the additions bear the marks of dates belonging to later months.

[E] According to the showing of the science of biblical criticism there is more than one Jesus of whom we have an account in the New Testament: (1) a naturalistic, this-worldly, pacific, human Jesus, and (2) a supernaturalistic, other-worldly, belligerent, divine Jesus, the Jesus of orthodox Christians.

[F] This shall be true of Marxian socialism when it is triumphant, but it will not be so while it is persecuted. Socialist Russia has asked for peace after every war which the capitalist nations (England, France, Italy and America) have waged against her, not because she could no longer defend herself, but for the reason that her socialism, being co-operative in its character, necessarily imposes humaneness; yet they could not grant it, because their capitalism, being competitive in its character, as necessarily imposes inhumaneness. The hand of the capitalist world is aggressively against socialist Russia, and must be, because the life of capitalism depends upon her death: and her hand is defensively against all the capitalist nations. Capitalism and socialism cannot occupy the earth together. Either the one or the other must have all of it. Mankind in general is illustrating the truth of the proverb which has been illustrated by so many families in particular—a house divided against itself cannot stand.

[Pg 82]

THE GRAND MARCH

By Helen Keller

The hour has struck for the Grand March! Onward, Comrades, all together! Fall in line! Start the New Year with a cheer! Let us join the world's procession marching toward a glad tomorrow. Strong of hope and brave in heart the West shall meet the East! March with us, brothers every one! March with us to all things new! Climb with us the hills of God to a wider, holier life. Onward, Comrades, all together, onward to meet the Dawn!

Leave behind you doubts and fears! What need have we for "ifs" and "buts"? Away with parties, schools and leagues! Get together, keep in step, shoulder to shoulder, hearts throbbing as one! Face the future, out-daring all you have dared! March on, O Comrades, strong and free, out of darkness, out of silence, out of hate and custom's deadening sway! Onward, Comrades, all together, onward to the wind-blown Dawn!

With us shall go the New Day, shining behind the dark. With us shall go Power, Knowledge, Justice, Truth. The time is full! A new world awaits us. Its fruits, its joys, its opportunities are ours for the taking! Fear not the hardships of the road—the storm, the parching heat or winter's cold, hunger or thirst or ambushed foe! There are bright lights ahead of us, leave the shadows behind! In the East a new star is risen! With pain and anguish the Old Order has given birth to the New, and behold, in the East a man-child is born! Onward, Comrades, all together! Onward to the camp-fires of Russia! Onward to the coming Dawn!

Through the night of our despair rings the keen call of the New Day. All the powers of darkness could not still that shout of joy in far-away Moscow! Meteor-like through the heavens flashed the golden words of light, "Soviet Republic of Russia". Words sun-like piercing the dark, joyous radiant love-words banishing hate, bidding the teeming world of men to wake and live! Onward, Comrades, all together, onward to the bright, redeeming Dawn!

With peace and brotherhood make sweet the bitter way of men! Today, and all the days to come, repeat the Word of Him who said, "Thou shall not kill". Send on psalming winds the angel-chorus, "Peace on earth, good-will to men". Onward march, and keep on marching until His Will on earth is done! Onward, Comrades, all together, onward to the life-giving fountain of Dawn!

All along the road beside us throng the peoples sad and broken, weeping women, children hungry, homeless like little birds cast out of their nest. With their hearts aflame, untamed, glorying in martyrdom they hail us passing quickly, "Halt not, O Comrades, yonder glimmers the star of our hope, the red-centered dawn in the East! Halt not, lest you perish ere you reach the Land of Promise". Onward, Comrades, all together, onward to the sun-red Dawn!

[Pg 83]

KARL MARX

[Pg 84]

CHARLES DARWIN

[Pg 85]

COMMUNISM AND CHRISTIANISM

ANALYZED AND CONTRASTED FROM THE MARXIAN AND DARWINIAN POINTS OF VIEW

PART II.

Christianism: A Supernaturalistic Other-worldly Gospel for the Passing Age of Class Inequality and Economic Slavery—An Open Letter to a Christian Theologian and Brother Churchman.

**Revolutionize capitalism out of
state and orthodoxy out of church.**

[Pg 86]

FOREWORD [G]

The contradiction in terms known as the Christian Socialist is inevitably antagonistic to working-class interests and the waging of the class struggle. His policy (that of the Christian Socialist) is the conciliation of classes, the fraternity of robber and robbed, not the end of classes. His avowed object, indeed, is usually to purge the Socialist movement of its materialism, and this means to purge it of its Socialism and to divert it from its material aims to the fruitless chasing of spiritual will-o'-the-wisps. A Christian Socialist is, in fact, an anti-Socialist.

Clearly, then, the basis of Socialist philosophy is utterly incompatible with religious ideas; indeed, the latter have been reduced to their logical absurdity in what is called "Christian Science."

Moreover, the consistent Christian, if such exists, could look upon the existing world only as an essential part of God's plan, to be accounted for only through God, and modified at God's pleasure. He could regard those who sought the explanation of social conditions in purely natural causes, and who also sought to take advantage of economic development in order to turn this vale of tears into a pleasant garden, only as men who denied by their acts the very basis of his faith.

FOOTNOTES:

[G] From the Official Manifesto by the Socialist Party of Great Britain, showing the Antagonism between Socialism and Religion.

[Pg 87]

CHRISTIANISM: A SUPERNATURALISTIC OTHER-WORLDLY GOSPEL FOR THE PASSING AGE OF CLASS INEQUALITY AND ECONOMIC SLAVERY.

Come over and help us.
Abandon Reformatory for
Revolutionary Socialism.

My Dear Brother:

Your letter (April 1st, 1920) enclosing an essay, entitled, Is There a God, came duly to hand and I thank you warmly for it. The essay is a masterpiece and I hope you can let me keep this copy, or make another for myself, for reference when I am writing or conversing on its lines, as is frequently the case.

I.

In the dispute between yourself and friend of which you speak, you are altogether right and he is entirely wrong. In the last analysis it is a disputation as to whether or not the Jewish-Christian bible contains an infallible revelation from an omniscient being, a triune god, Father, Son and Spirit. It does not.

As an objectivity there is no such divinity. He is a subjectivity existing in the imagination of orthodox Christians. You do not agree with me in this, but every day of thought and study deepens the conviction that it is true. None among the gods of the supernaturalistic interpretations of religion are objectivities. The lesser ones are generally ghosts of dead [Pg 88] men, and the greater ones are as generally versions of the sun-myth.

The one god of the Jews and the triune god of the Christians, if taken seriously, are superstitions; and the bible revelations of their willings and records of their doings, if taken literally, are lies.

Both the Old and New Testaments are utterly worthless as history. The twelve patriarchs of the Jewish God, Jehovah, are not historical personages, but myths, and this is true of the twelve apostles of the Christian God, Jesus.

Yes, the Old Testament is the Jewish version of the immemorial and universal sun-myth, rewritten several times for the purpose, not of telling any truth, but of imposing the fiction that Jehovah and his people constitute the greatest procession that ever came down the pike of supernaturalism. The New Testament is the Christian version of the same myth, only with the view of showing that Jehovah and the Jews were not, but Jesus and Christians are, this procession.

In itself, the sun-myth, as symbolism, is not only poetically beautiful, but also scientifically true; yet, as literalism, it is in the case of the ignorant, superstition, and in the case of the educated, self-deception.

The sun is, in a very literal and real sense, the creator-god in whom this world lives, moves and has its being; and he is the saviour-god who was born of a virgin nebula, and every winter descends into hell and rises from the dead (the southern solstice) by a new birth and ascends into heaven to be seated at the right hand of the father (the sky) at the northern solstice, and finally he is the illuminator god who lighteth every man that cometh into the world. [Pg 89]

And the apostles who preached the gospel of the redemption of the world are the twelve signs of the zodiac through which the sun apparently passes in its annual ascension to the summer solstice and descension to the winter solstice.

Nor is this all: "the Lamb of God that taketh away the sins of the world" is the sign of the zodiac, Aries (sheep, ram) through which the sun passes towards the end of March, when all the saviour-gods annually died and rose again. The rising symbolizes the return of the sun towards the northern solstice from the southern one, upon which return seed-time and harvest are dependent, without which the world would perish, not indeed by sin but by starvation.

Jehovah is the sun-myth rewritten to fit in with the ideals and hopes of the owning, master class of the Jews.

Jesus is the sun-myth rewritten to fit in with the ideals and hopes of the owning master class of the Christians.

The Christian god, Jesus, is an improvement upon the Jewish god, Jehovah, because of the division of labor. The task of the owning master class is a twofold one, the robbing of the weak owners by the strong ones in wars, and the robbing of the slaves by the masters which under the capitalist system is done in surplus profits.

Jehovah serves Christians as the god of war. In his name they wage wars, either as groups within a nation having different commercial interests, as in the case of the Civil War of the United States, or as nations against nations with different commercial interests, as in the case of the Revolutionary war of the [Pg 90] Colonies with England, or the World War of the Allied countries with the Central ones.

Jesus serves Christians as the god of slavery. When they have successfully waged a war of conquest, as the Pilgrim Fathers did against the Indians of America, or when they have appropriated all the means and machines of production, as the capitalists have everywhere, they reconcile the propertyless to a terrestrial hell of toil, want, sorrow and slavery by preaching the Jesuine gospel of hope for a celestial heaven of eternal rest, joy, plenty and freedom.

> "Some for the Glories of This World; and some Sigh for the Prophet's Paradise to come; Ah, take the Cash, and let the Credit go, Nor heed the rumble of a distant Drum."

In remaking the Jewish god to suit their purposes of robbing and enslaving, the Christian owning master class provided for a further division of his work by creating the Holy Ghost, who devotes himself to the giving of new revelations of the will of Jehovah and interpreting the earlier ones as they are recorded in the bible.

It is generally supposed that the masters are the strong people of the world, but they are not. Labor is really the giant, the Samson, and it would be impossible for the pigmy, capital, to rob him, but for his lack of knowledge. The Holy Ghost sees to it that the slave class is kept in ignorance.

The English-German, or if you prefer, the German-English war has been an eye-opener to the giant, labor, and capital is ruined unless he can get him to sleep again. [Pg 91]

Capital knows that Marx was right in characterizing the orthodox interpretations of religion, including the Christian one, and especially it, as a sleeping potion.

The churches were the dormitories in which the slaves slept through the night of the dark ages of traditionalism, but the light of the age of scientism is breaking upon the world and most of the slaves have left the churches and are now beyond the reach of their care-takers, the preachers.

When I wrote the Level Plan for Church Union, I believed that the coming together of the churches would prove to be a blessing to the world, but I am now persuaded that it would be a curse, because the league of churches would co-operate with the league of nations in its robbing and enslaving schemes, the churches doing the lying and the nations the coercing.

We are living in the age of scientism and, in the case of its true sons and daughters, only scientifically demonstrated facts count in any argumentation.

From the scientific point of view it is seen that there is but one universal Kingdom of Life, Nature. This kingdom may be divided into three, perhaps four, states constituting the United States of Life: the mineral, the vegetable, the animal and the human.

Beginning with the highest, each of these states, except the lowest, is dependent upon the next lower. The only independent autonomous state in the kingdom is the mineral. This is the greatest both as to its extent and importance. It is the common source of every supply of all the states of life, and the seat of each of their governments.

All theologians and some metaphysicians postulate [Pg 92] a fifth state of life, the divine, placing it above the rest as their source.

Comte, who preceded Marx as a social philosopher, and who is the founder of modern socialism of the reformatory type, as Marx is of the revolutionary one, had this to say about the theologians, metaphysicians and scientists, and he was right:

From the study of the development of human intelligence, in all directions, and through all times, the discovery arises of a great fundamental law, to which it is necessarily subject, and which has a solid foundation of proof, both in the facts of our organization and in our historical experience. This law is this: that each of our leading conceptions—each branch of our knowledge—passes successively through three different theoretical conditions: the theological, or fictitious; the metaphysical, or abstract; and the scientific, or positive. In other words, the human mind, by its nature, employs in its progress three methods of philosophizing, the character of which is essentially different and radically opposed: viz., the theological method, the metaphysical and the positive. Hence arise three philosophies, or general systems of conceptions on the aggregate of phenomena, each of which excludes the others. The first is the necessary point of departure of the human understanding; the third is its fixed and definite state. The second is merely a state of transition.

In order for a man who has reached the scientific stage in his intellectual development to make anything out of the reasonings of those who are still in the stage of theological childhood or in that of metaphysical adolescence, it is necessary for him to use their insubstantialities as symbols of his substantialities.

The only difference that I can see between a theologian and a metaphysician is that, whereas the former [Pg 93] personifies a generality which is the creation of his imagination, calling it a god, the latter objectifies a particularity which is the creation of his imagination calling it an entity; but all such personifications and objectifications (gods, things-in-themselves, vital entities, souls) are alike fictitious, because the childish theologians and metaphysicians proceed on the basis of philosophically assumed realities, not on scientifically established facts which pave the way on which an adult proceeds.

Comte analyzes the difference between the intellectuality of theological children, metaphysical youths and scientific adults as follows:

In the theological state, the human mind, seeking the essential nature of beings, the first and final causes (the origin and purpose) of all effects—in short, absolute knowledge—supposes all phenomena to be produced by the immediate action of supernatural beings.

In the metaphysical state, which is only a modification of the first, the mind supposes, instead of supernatural beings, abstract forces, veritable entities (that is, personified abstractions) inherent in all beings, and capable of producing all phenomena. What is called the explanation of phenomena is, in this stage, a mere reference of each to its proper entity.

In the final, the positive state, the mind has given over the vain search after absolute notions, the origin and destination of the universe, and the causes of phenomena, and applies itself to the study of their laws—that is, their invariable relations of succession and resemblance. Reasoning and observation, duly combined, are the means of this knowledge. What is now understood when we speak of an explanation of facts is simply the establishment of a connection be [Pg 94] tween single phenomena and some general facts the number of which continually diminishes with the progress of science.

There is no science which, having attained the positive stage, does not bear the marks of having passed through the others. Some time since it was (whatever it might be now) composed, as we can now perceive, of metaphysical abstractions: and, further back in the course of time, it took its form from theological conceptions. Our most advanced sciences still bear very evident marks of the two earlier periods through which they passed.

The progress of the individual mind is not only an illustration, but an indirect evidence of that of the general mind. The point of departure of the individual and the race being the same, the phases of the mind of men correspond to the epochs of the mind of the race. How each of us is aware, if he looks back upon his own history, that he was a theologian in his childhood, a metaphysician in his youth and a natural philosopher in his manhood. All men who are up to their age can verify this for themselves.

According to the scientific classification, there are only three kingdoms or states of life, the mineral, the vegetable and the animal.

The life of the vegetable kingdom has arisen out of the life of the mineral kingdom and is sustained by it.

The distinguished scientist, Professor Lowell, says, "there is now no more reason to doubt that plants grew out of chemical affinity than to doubt that stones did," and nearly all outstanding zoologists would say as much of animals.

Sir J. Burdon Sanderson, one of the most eminent among biologists, insists that "in physiology the word life is understood to mean the chemical and physical activities of the parts of which the organism consists." [Pg 95] The renowned Sir Ray Lankester strenuously holds that "zoology is the science which seeks to arrange and discuss the phenomena of animal life and form, as the outcome of the operation of the laws of physics and chemistry," and goes so far as to say that he knows of no leading biologist who is of a different opinion. The prince of biologists, the late Professor Haeckel, occupied this position and impregnably fortified it in several great books, especially in his "Riddle of the Universe."

There is no force that is not life, nor life which is not force; and there is no life or force, about which we know anything, without a body or chemical laboratory.

So far as is known, there is only one life—force. The difference between lives is a question of the organism, the laboratory, which gives embodiment to force.

The life that enables the wheels of a locomotive to go, the sap of a tree to flow, the heart of an animal to beat and the brain of a man to think is the same chemical potentiality differently organized.

During all historical time and over all the earth, under one name or another, the whole world has kept days of rejoicing for life, especially Thanksgiving, Christmas, New Year and Easter.

Nothing is so wonderful as life and perhaps the greatest of its wonders is that all of it is of the same kind.

Everything and every being is alive with the same life. The Thanksgiving day sheaf of wheat, the Christmas day Son of Man and the Easter day Son of God (if there are conscious, personal gods and they [Pg 96] have sons) are alive and their life is the same, the difference being wholly in the form and degree, not at all in kind.

A proof of the oneness and sameness of all life, notwithstanding its widely different forms and degrees, is the fact that a bar of iron, a stick of wood, a piece of flesh and a section of brain respond alike to the same electrical stimulus, and all may be poisoned or otherwise killed so that they will make no response to it. Perhaps even a more conclusive evidence is that the eggs (every form of both vegetable and animal life develops from an egg) of some animals rather high in the one tree of mundane life, which has a common root and a stump, but two stems, the vegetable and the animal, can be mechanically fertilized by chemical processes.

Even Sir Oliver Lodge, the most conspicuous among the comparatively few men of science who hold to the theory that life comes to the earth as vital entities of celestial origin and destination, makes this fatal admission: "There is plenty of physics and chemistry and mechanics about every vital action." On the theory of traditional Christianity there was no physics, chemistry or mechanics connected with the vital actions which originally brought the universe and all that therein was, including the earth with its vegetable, animal and human kingdoms, into existence.

Every representative of each form of life in these kingdoms (in the vegetable: a grass blade, a wheat stalk, an oak tree; or in the animal: an insect, a horse, a man) is a chemical laboratory for the production, sustentation, advancement and procreation of a particular type of one universal life. These laboratories [Pg 97] have all the potentialities of their respective lives within themselves,—no laboratory, no chemistry; no chemistry, no life.

What life is, both as to its manifestation and character, is determined by the form of organization through which force, all there is of life, becomes a particular and differentiated vital phenomenon. This is as true of states and churches as it is of trees and men, for a church or a state is a vital phenomenon as really so as a tree or a man.

The trouble with every reformatory socialism of modern times is that it undertakes the impossibility of changing the fruit of the capitalistic state into that of the communistic one, without changing the political organism; but to do that is as impossible as to gather grapes from thorns or figs from thistles. Hence an uprooting and replanting are necessary (a revolution not a reformation) which will give the world a new tree of state.

Capitalism no longer grows the fruits (foods, clothes and houses) which are necessary to the sustenance of the world. Hence it encumbers the ground and must be dug up by the roots in order that a tree which is so organized that it will bear these necessities may be planted in its place.

The people of Russia have accomplished this uprooting and replanting (this revolution) in the case of their state, and those of every nation are destined to do the same in one way or another, each according to its historical and economic development, some perhaps with violence, most, I hope, peaceably. The Russian Bolsheviki occupy the highest peak in man's history; and while they stand, the world will [Pg 98] be safe for industrial democracy. This democracy is the tree of life whose fruits are for the sustenance of the nations and whose very leaves are for their healing.

The only lives of which we need know aught are those that we shall live in our bodies by chemical processes and in the race by conscious or unconscious influences; for, if there is another, it will take care of itself, if we take care of these.

Since, therefore, all life is on a level and since morality, religion and Christianity are but manifestations of it, do you not see how profoundly and incontrovertibly true is my levelism?

According to this levelism all interpretations of Christianity (protestant and catholic—congregational, presbyterian, episcopalian and papal) and all the interpretations of religion (Christian, Jewish, Mohammedan, Buddhistic and the rest) are essentially on the same footing, the difference between them being wholly a question of natural excellencies, not at all of supernatural uniqueness.

The science of biology establishes my levelism by proving that animal and human life are on a level as to their origin, character and destiny.

The science of sociology establishes my levelism by proving that animal and human institutions are on a level, and that therefore, there is nothing more supernatural about a human state or church than about an ant hill or a bee hive.

The science of literary criticism establishes my levelism by proving that the bibles of the several interpretations of religion are on a level as to their entirely human origin and authority. [Pg 99]

The science of the comparative interpretations of religion establishes my levelism by proving that all the conscious, personal creator-gods, destroyer-gods, saviour-gods and illuminator-gods, with all their angels, heavens and hells, are so many myths—creations of the human imagination, subjective fictions, not objective realities.

Until comparatively recent times, through all the theological history of mankind, the sun was almost universally regarded as a god. Manifestly without it there could be no life on earth, and its annually recurring motions are such as to give the impression of birth and death—of birth by ascension into the heaven of the summer solstice—of death by descension into the hell or grave of the winter solstice. Not only is the sun the giver and sustainer of life, but it is also the light that lighteth every man that cometh into the world.

Modern science justifies this ancient conception as to the dependence of the earth, and all that thereon is, upon the sun for its being. By a slight adaptation men of science and scientific philosophers could use the very words of the apostle John at the opening of his version of the Christian gospel, where he says of Jesus, what they say of the sun:

All things were made by him and without him was not anything made that was made. In him is life; and the life is the light of men.

The birth, death, descension, resurrection and ascension of all the Saviour-gods, not excepting Jesus, are versions of the sun-myth.

Yet the naturalness, the universalness, the beautifulness and withal the profound truthfulness of this myth are such as to render it almost as undesirable [Pg 100] as it is next to impossible to relegate it to the realm of superstition, to which it should undoubtedly be assigned if a literal interpretation is a necessity.

The more science advances, the more of precious poetry and pathos, and of deep verity, too, is seen in the Saviour-gods, who are essentially the same mythical personifications of the glorious sun and of the happy events of its annual career, because from it the earth with its brother and sister planets had their origin, and because from it the earth, not to speak of the other planets, has the heat, light and force which make its life a possibility.

There is no reason for believing that any one among the gods of the four old supernaturalistic interpretations of religion (Jehovah, Jesus, Allah, Buddha) or that either of the gods of the two new interpretations by the renowned physicist, Sir Oliver Lodge, and the distinguished sociologist, Mr. H. G. Wells, has had more to do in creating, sustaining and governing this world than another, that is to say, there is no ground for believing that the personal, conscious gods in the skies either individually or collectively have had anything at all to do with it.

Science, as it is understood by the great majority of its exponents, teaches that the earth (with all things, physical and psychical, which contribute to make its world what it has been, is, and is to be) was originally in the sun, and would quickly disappear into its original, unorganized elements but for the sun.

This is as true of man as of all else. He with his brain and its thought, with his hand and its skill; with his homes, farms, cities, mines, shops, stores, trains, ships, schools, hospitals and churches; with his hate, bestiality and barbarism, and with his love, hu [Pg 101] maneness and civilization, was in the sun, billions of years before his appearance on the earth.

Speaking of things appertaining to the world war: there in the sun, before it had thrown off the earth, were the kaiser on the throne, the president in the white house, the millions of soldiers, the uniforms, the rations, the forts, the cannons, guns, powder and shot, the trenches, the barbed wire, the dreadnoughts, the submarines, the aeroplanes, the wireless telegraph stations, the wounded, their sufferings and groans, the doctors and nurses, the corpses, the cripples, the broken hearts; yes, and all the things connected with that terrible war; the bereaved mothers, the widowed wives, the outraged girls, the ruined country, the wrecked cities, were in the sun from its beginning, indeed while it was yet a nebula, many thousands of millions of years previous to the birth of the earth.

If we except intruders into our solar system, such as comets and their comparatively inconsiderable effects, we may say that every physical or psychical reality which at any time has entered into the history of this planet and that of its brothers and sisters was in that vast flowing, swirling, revolving globe of gases which is known to have been at one time at least five billion miles in diameter, or fifteen billions in circumference.

Of course no phenomenon, such as Jesus hanging on the cross, if He lived and was crucified, was in the sun as an actuality, but only as a potentiality. Nevertheless He, with His doctrine and His suffering, was there, else He would never have been anywhere, not in the realm of history, not even in the realm of imagination.

The universe is ever all that it can be, and every po [Pg 102] tentiality which contributes to make it so is within itself. What is true in this respect of the universe as a whole is equally so of every part of it, including man, and especially him, because he is exceptionally capable of controlling his own destiny, being able not only to preserve life by a discovery of and conformity to the laws upon which it is dependent, but also to enlarge and enrich its content by making these laws co-operative servants.

The time cannot be far off when it will be seen by all educated, thoughtful men and women that if the traditional, supernaturalistic interpretation of Christianity is the only possible one, its message is not a gospel, because its teaching touching three fundamentals is, in each case, contrary to that of three relevant sciences:

1. The sciences of astronomy, geology and biology teach that the representation of traditional supernaturalistic interpretation of Christianity to the effect that the universe, including the earth with its physical and psychical life, was supernaturally created out of nothing by a conscious, personal god is not true and therefore can be no part of any gospel; for, according to the teaching of these three sciences, the truth is: the universe with all that therein is, not excepting mankind and civilization, was naturally evolved out of a self-existing matter by a self-existing force co-operating in accordance with the necessity of their nature.

2. The sciences of biology, physiology and embryology teach that the representation of the traditional, supernaturalistic interpretation of Christianity to the effect that man and woman are unique beings, who have supernaturally derived their physical form, vital [Pg 103] and psychical potentialities directly from a conscious, personal crea-

tor with whom are their natural affiliations, is not true, and therefore can be no part of any gospel; for, according to the teaching of these three sciences, the truth is: man and woman as to their whole beings (body and mind, life and soul) were naturally evolved from pre-existing animal life, not supernaturally created respectively out of the dust and a rib, so that they owe their existence to and natural affinities with a terrestrial and bestial parentage, not a celestial and divine one.

3. The sciences of anthropology, sociology and comparative interpretations of religion teach that the representation of the traditional, supernaturalistic interpretation of Christianity to the effect that man and woman were supernaturally created in the image and likeness of a conscious, personal god, sinless and deathless beings with ideal environments, but that they fell from this happy estate, through a serpentine incarnation of a supernatural devil, and are being restored to it, through a human incarnation of a supernatural saviour, is not true, and therefore can be no part of any gospel; for, according to the teaching of these three sciences, the truth is: during many ages man and woman, in both appearance and predilection, were much more animal than divine and that gradually, without any supernatural assistance, they have worked themselves out of a state of bestial barbarism into one of human civilization.

It follows therefore that the representations of both the Old and New Testaments, concerning the origin and history of man are largely fictitious impositions, not historical compositions, so much so, that no confidence can safely be reposed in any of them. [Pg 104]

There is no rational doubt about the fictitious character of the divine Jesus. Some think that the human Jesus may have been an historical personage; but, none among outstanding scholars believes that we have a connected account of his life and work, and most of them insist that we do not certainly know any saying or doing of his.

No religious doctrine or institution of which we have an account in the New Testament is peculiar to Christianity and this is equally true of moral precepts.

The gods of all the supernaturalistic interpretations of religion are so many creations of the dominant or master class, and their revelations were put into their mouths by the makers for the purpose of keeping the slave class ignorant and contented.

Orthodox Christians earnestly contend that this naturalistic doctrine makes for immorality. Heretical socialists rationally answer that the life which men, women and children live with reference to their terrestrial influence, rather than to celestial rewards or punishments, is the only one which is lived to any moral purpose.

According to socialism, morality, religion and Christianity are but synonyms of one and the same reality, which consists wholly in the desire and effort of a man to learn the laws or doings of nature, and to conform his thoughts and words to them, in order to make his present life on earth, and that of others, as long and happy as possible, and not at all in a desire and effort to learn what the will of a conscious, personal god is and to conform to it, in order to avoid a hell and gain a heaven for a future life in the sky. [Pg 105]

> O threats of Hell and Hopes of Paradise! One thing at least is certain—This Life flies; One thing is certain and the rest is Lies; The Flower that once has blown forever dies.

If you object that this is a representation of a sceptical poet, I reply that it is in alignment with a representation of a scriptural preacher:

> For that which befalleth the sons of men befalleth beasts; Even one thing befalleth them; As the one dieth, so dieth the other; Yea, they have all one breath; So that a man hath no pre-eminence above a beast; For all is vanity. All go unto one place; All are of the dust, And all turn to dust again.

Darwin showed that each man in his physical development from the embryonic cell to birth passes through, by short cuts, the different forms of life from say, the worm, fish and lemur with all that went before, intervened between and followed after, and Romanes showed that this is as true of the mind as of the body; that, in fact, all the representatives of the animal kingdom are physically and psychically related, and therefore on the same level as to their origin and destiny.

In his illuminating book entitled, "The Universal Kinship," Professor Moore says:

The embryonic development of a human being is no different from the embryonic development of any other animal. Every human being at the beginning of his organic existence is a protozoan, about 1-125 inch [Pg 106] in diameter; at another stage of development he is a tiny sac-shaped mass of cells without blood or nerves, the gastrula; at another stage he is a worm, with a pulsating tube instead of a heart, and without a head, neck, spinal column, or limbs; at another stage he has as a backbone, a rod of cartilage extending along the back, and a faint nerve cord, as in the amphioxus, the lowest of the vertebrates; at another stage he is a fish with a two-chambered heart, mesonephric kidneys, and gill-slits, with gill arteries leading to them, just as in fishes; at another stage he is a reptile with a three-chambered heart, and voiding his excreta through a cloaca like other reptiles; and finally, when he enters upon post-natal sins and actualities, he is a sprawling, squalling, unreasoning quadruped. The human larva from the fifth to the seventh month of development is covered with a thick growth of hair and has a true caudal (tail) appendage, like the monkey. At this stage the embryo has in all thirty-eight vertebrae, nine of which are caudal, and the great toe extends at right angles to the other toes, and is not longer than the other toes, but shorter, as in the ape.

Surely no argument is needed to convince you that Darwinism corroborates the representation of our ancient heretical poet and scriptural preacher concerning a life beyond the grave rather than the representations of modern orthodox theologians.

> Strange, is it not? that of the myriads who Before us pass'd the door of Darkness through, Not one returns to tell us of the Road, Which to discover we must travel, too.
> —Omar.

II.

In history slavery stands out as a huge mountain range traversing the whole of a continent. During [Pg 107] long ages it was supposed that these phenomena of the human and physical worlds were due to the will of a god (Jesus, Jehovah, Allah or Buddha) but the vanguard of humanity has now reached a viewpoint from which it sees that both are alike due to a law, that a law is what nature does, not what a god has willed, and that a system of slavery and a range of mountains are due to the same law.

The matter-force law is everywhere the same, and it is as omnipotent and immutable in a social order as in a solar system.

> "The very law that moulds a tear, And bids it trickle from its source, That law preserves the earth a sphere, And guides the planets in their course."

Most of the time, and especially just now, our world is very full of tears, almost as much so as space is full of spheres, but there would not be half so many tears at any time, if the laws of states were so many correct interpretations of the laws of nature.

In every age, nearly all the hot tears which deluge the world flow, like streams of springs, from their deep sources as the result of unnecessary suffering by grinding poverty, by hopeless slavery, by avoidable diseases and by premature deaths; and by far the most of these and of all sufferings may be traced to man-made laws which not only have no correspondence with those of nature but are contrary to them—laws of which both the civil codes and religious bibles are too full.

You will agree with me that society should punish none of its members by the slightest fine or shortest imprisonment, not to speak of death, except on the [Pg 108] basis of justice. So far, and it is a long way, we certainly walk together. We part company, if at all, on the question as to the basis of justice, but come together again in the conclusion that it is right, not might.

What, then, is this right? If you answer: the law of the state as it is interpreted by a competent court, I reply: no legal enactment, and so, of course, no interpretation of one, can really constitute a right, unless it is an embodiment of a truth containing an indispensable stone in the foundation which is necessary to the superstructure of the ideal civilization, under the roof of which every man, woman and child shall possess the greatest of possible opportunities to make life for self as long and happy as it can be, and to help others in an ever widening circle to do this for themselves.

Laws are not made. All social laws (domestic, civil, commercial, yes, even the moral and religious ones) are matter-force realities, as much so as is any other among all the physical or psychical realities entering into the constitution of the universe; which realities are but the expressions of the processes necessarily resulting from the necessary co-existence and co-operation of this matter and force; therefore, laws are so many eternal necessities and, this being the case, it is not possible that men in states or churches should make them, no, not even gods in heavens.

Man would, then, have progressed much further with the superstructure of an ideal civilization, if only in his efforts to rightly regulate his life, he had happily searched out the laws of nature as they are revealed through its phenomena and interpreted by experience and reason, instead of looking for direction [Pg 109] to the laws of the gods (Jehovah, Allah, Buddha or even Jesus) as they are revealed through prophets and interpreted by kings or presidents, by priests or preachers and by other "powers that be of God" in states and churches—institutions which exist in the interest of the capitalist class and against that of the labor class. The world owes by far the greater part of its most poignant sufferings to this fatal mistake of looking to gods in heavens and their representatives on earth for direction instead of to nature and reason.

Life in the physical realm is dependent upon living in harmony with the matter-force law. The representative of any form of life (mineral, vegetable, animal, human) which either through ignorance, accident or willfulness does not conform to it, is destroyed or at least injured.

Life in the moral part of the psychical realm consists in a disposition and effort to learn the matter-force law, and to fulfill in thought, word and deed the individual obligations to self and the social obligations to others imposed by it when it has been humanely interpreted by a man for himself.

Religion and Christianity are but wider extensions of one and the same great all-inclusive virtue, morality, without which human life would not be worth living, indeed not even a possibility, for without morality a man is a beast, not a human.

Morality is the greatest thing in the world. Yet, paradoxical as the representation may seem, there is one greater thing, freedom—the liberty to think, speak and act in accordance with one's own convictions as to what is the law and as to what are its requirements. Without this liberty there could be no morality, and [Pg 110] therefore, freedom is greater than the greatest thing in the world, morality.

But liberty, the greatest and most indispensable necessity to morality, religion and Christianity, indeed, to the existence of a human being, is manifestly impossible on the theory that a man must be guided by the will of a conscious, personal God in the sky as it is interpreted by the kings and priests, presidents and preachers on earth.

You will note that I am not contending for the liberty to live without reference to an external authority. If this were my contention you would rightly insist (as some among my friends do) that I am an atheist in religion and an anarchist in politics; but I am neither, for I recognize the fact that I must live with reference to the existence of an external authority, matter-force law, and there is no other, upon which anything good in religion or politics is dependent.

No one is an atheist in religion, an anarchist in politics or anything bad, who, in the physical realm of life, tries to live with reference to the law of nature, and who, in the moral realm of life, tries to live with reference to a truth which is that law humanely interpreted by himself in accordance with his own experience, observation, investigation and reason. In the nature of things, the interpretation cannot be by some one else, because one man cannot live the moral life on another's ideals any more than he can live the physical life on another's meals.

Since this is the case, it follows that the whole conception of a law which is willed by a god and revealed or formulated by his representatives (prophets, kings, priests, legislators) to which a man must have refer [Pg 111] ence, if he would live the moral life, is, at best, a harmless fiction and at worst a hurtful superstition.

There is no one (man or god) with whom people can stand in the moral realm except themselves alone, and if they are not within this realm they are not men and women.

Manhood is dependent upon standing alone with matter-force nature and with human reason, and it is manhood which really counts everywhere in the social realm, for without manhood one is nothing anywhere in that realm.

Nature is my God. The gods of the several supernaturalistic interpretations of religion (Jesus, Jehovah, Allah, Buddha) are so many symbols of this divinity. The words of this God are the facts of nature. My religion and politics, worship and patriotism consist in a desire and effort to discover these facts and to interpret and live them humanely.

My God, Nature, is a triune divinity—matter being the Father, force the Son, and law the Spirit.

Nature is the sum of the matter-force-law phenomena of which the universe is constituted. Man with his barbarism and civilization is but one among such phenomena, on a level with the rest, as to his beginning and ending, and as to the dependence of his life and its fullness upon conformity to the matter-force law, without necessary or, indeed, possible reference to any divine-human system of laws as set forth by a catholic or protestant church or by an imperialistic or democratic state.

Unless states and churches persuade, encourage and help man to more fully discover, more correctly interpret and more perfectly live the matter-force law they are worthless; and indeed worse, if in the long run [Pg 112] and on the whole they hinder him; and undoubtedly they have done this in the case of the slave class—a class which, ever since the rise of private property in the means of producing the necessities of life, has comprehended the vast majority of the human race.

Whether then man is barbarous or civilized is really and truly, wholly and entirely a question of the knowledge of and conformity to the matter-force law, that is, of whether or not the articles of his religious creed and political code are so many ideal embodiments and practical interpretations of facts or realities as they are revealed by the doings of my god, Nature.

There is no other creed, belief in the articles of which, and there is no other code, obedience to the articles of which, will advance mankind, individually or collectively, so much as one step in the long, rugged and steep way towards the goal of a perfect civilization—a civilization which will secure to every man, woman and child the greatest of possible opportunities to make the most of life that is within the range of possibilities.

My god, Nature (the triune divinity, matter-force-motion) the doings of which god are so many words of the only gospel upon which the salvation of the world is to any degree dependent, is an impersonal, unconscious, non-moral being.

For me, this god, Nature, rises into personality, consciousness and morality in myself, and in no other does nature do this for me, though what is true of me is of course equally so of every representative of mankind.

Jesus (either as an historical or dramatic personage, and it does not matter which he was) said, "I and my Father (god) are one," and in saying this he gave expression in one form to the most revolutionary and salu [Pg 113] tary of all truths. The other form of the same truth as taught by Darwin and Marx is: man has all the potentialities of his own life within himself. Every representative of the human race can and should say with Jesus, "I and my Father, God, are one."

> Stop man! where dost thou run? Heav'n lies within thy heart,
> If thou seek'st God elsewhere Misled, in truth, thou art.
> —Angelus Silensius.

This truth constitutes the most ennobling and inspiring part of man's knowledge, and it was naturally discovered by him, not supernaturally revealed to him. It is the foundation of socialism and the justification of optimism.

The universe moves, with all that therein is. The vanguard of mankind is moving to a viewpoint from which rapidly increasing numbers will see that a revolution which is necessary on the part of a slave to free himself from a master is not only justified but required by the great, first law of the biological realm, the law of self-preservation—a nature-made law on behalf of freedom. This nature-made law will ultimately nullify all class laws, every law which is in favor of the enslaving capitalist class and against the enslaved labor class.

Every state with its executive, legislative, judiciary, military and educative systems is founded on capitalism. Since this is the case and since human nature is what it is, all political institutions, the American with the rest, are of the capitalist, by the capitalist, for the capitalist, and each to the end that the capitalist may keep the laborer in poverty and slavery. [Pg 114]

Every modern church with its ministry, bible, creed, heaven and hell is founded on capitalism. Since this is the case, and since human nature is what it is, all religious institutions, the Christian with the rest, are of the capitalist, by the capitalist, for the capitalist and each to the end that the capitalist may keep the laborer in ignorance and slavery.

Whether Jesus was an historical or a dramatic person, the morality involved in his trial, condemnation and execution is the same. Assuming the historicity, he was put to death by Pilate because a class of the people said: We have a law and by it, according to its official interpretation, he should die. The Governor, finding that the legal enactment and the judicial decision were in accordance with the representation of the Jews, turned Jesus over to the executioners for crucifixion, and the world condemns him because he knew that the law was the embodiment of a fiction instead of a truth, because he interpreted it in the interest of a sect instead of a people, and because he basely acted with reference to his own political interests without regard to justice for an heroic but helpless champion of slaves in their struggle against the masters.

Philosophic anarchy differs by the space of the whole heavens from practical anarchy, and it is the latter that I always have in mind. The great essential of philosophic anarchy is individualistic freedom. The great essential of practical anarchy is imperialistic slavery.

Capitalism is the outstanding, overshadowing imperialist, the father of all the kaisers by which the world has been cursed, not only of the terrestrial ones such as Wilhelm II, Nicholas II, Woodrow I, but also of the celestial ones such as Jehovah, Allah, Buddha. [Pg 115]

The occupants of regal thrones have no more responsibility for the existence of imperialism than those of presidential chairs, nor they any more than I, and I have none. The truth is that the responsibility for this blight of all the ages is now at last, if indeed it has not always been, wholly with the representatives of the working class. They have the great majority in numbers and all of the revolutionary incentives and power; therefore they, and only they can do away with imperialism, and they can rid themselves of it whenever they choose. Prince Kropotkin, the philosophic anarchist, a great soul, would agree to this representation, for he says:

The working men of the civilized world and their friends in the other classes ought to induce their Governments entirely to abandon the idea of armed intervention in the affairs of Russia—whether open or disguised, whether military or in the shape of subventions to different nations.

Russia is now living through a revolution of the same depth and the same importance as the British nation underwent in 1639-1648 and France in 1789-1794; and every nation should refuse to play the shameful part that Great Britain, Prussia, Austria and Russia played during the French Revolution.

Since death ends all of consciousness, the most inhuman of all inhumanities and the most immoral of all immoralities is the shortening of human life; and next to it is the diminishing of its happiness.

War shortens many lives and fills more with misery; hence its essential inhumanity and immorality.

A large part of the world has just passed through the furnace of war—a war between the German and English nations with their respective national allies. All international wars are contests for supremacy in the [Pg 116] markets of the world, or at least for advantage in some among them. This one was no exception.

The furnace of this war was seven times larger and seven times hotter than any other has been. According to the latest estimates (September, 1920) its fierce flames directly and indirectly killed thirty million young men and wrecked totally twice and partially thrice as many more.

Yet the fire by which the world upon the whole and in the long run suffers most is not the intermittent, flaming one of the hell of international war, which is always kindled and sustained by the capitalists of the belligerent nations for the purpose solely of securing commercial advantages over each other; but the greater suffering is by the permanent, smoking fire of the hell of the inter-class war which is always kindled and sustained by the capitalist class in each nation for the purpose solely of robbing the labor class of the fruit of their toil.

These national and class wars (hells, flaming and smouldering) are due to the same matter-force law, the law of self-preservation, and, paradoxical as it may seem, this law is equally operative on both sides in each war.

Both hells exist as the result of the working out of the same law of animal preservation by competition—the law of capitalism, and both hells will be done away with as the result of the working out of the same law of human preservation by co-operation—the law of socialism.

One proof of the rightness of the co-operative system is the fact that it necessarily operates for the whole people and not for a class, whereas the competi [Pg 117] tive system as necessarily operates for a class and not for the whole people.

Still another proof, and it is in itself almost if not quite conclusive, of the rightness of the co-operative system is the fact that its competitive rival breaks down in every great emergency. It broke down completely in all the belligerent countries (in none more than the United States) immediately upon their entrance into the world war. Our government was obliged to assume control of the railroads, coal mines and food products.

If a class government, such as ours is, can provide during a war by the co-operative system, and only by it, for the wants of a country, and better, too, than during the time of peace, what may we expect in the way of plenty, comfort and leisure, when under the classless administration there shall be no more war with its wholesale waste, and when there shall be one vast army of producers?

All the days which the fifty millions of soldiers spent in idleness will then be so many holidays for toilers who are in need of them for rest and self-improvement; and every dollar which is now wasted will then be two dollars saved, so that the pecuniary prosperity of war times will be increased, rather than diminished, and made continuous. Under a classless administration the world would soon become comparatively rich and happy. [H]

[Pg 118]

Representatives of the capitalist class are trying to create the impression that the co-operative system which our government temporarily established as a military necessity is socialism, and that the labor class should seek no more than its restoration and continuance: but this system is the same old wolf in sheep's clothing.

The rickety house in which we are living is a competitive structure and it cannot be made into a co-operative one, at least not upon its present foundation, the sand of capitalistic classism. Industrialism must take it down and rebuild it upon the rock of classless labor. Neither this demolition nor this reconstruction constitutes any part of the government program. Its socialism is a mirage, not a reality, and the matter-force law renders it necessarily so.

Marxian socialism is simplicity itself. It requires only three conditions, each of which is perfectly intelligible; but no one of them ever has existed or could exist under any capitalist government, because all such governments, not excepting our own, especially not it, are organized in the interest of parasitic profiteers, not productive laborers. The three indispensable yet simple prerequisites to this real socialism or communism are:

First, that the people within a municipality, either town or city, own and control the utilities within the area occupied by that municipality, which have to do with the immediate comfort of the people who live there.

Second, that the people in each state own and control the utilities that come in contact with the people on a state-wide scale.

Third, that the people within the nation own collectively and control democratically the utilities which affect us on a national scale. [Pg 119]

Should we desire to go into more detail, we might say that the things necessary to the individual be owned and controlled by the individual, that the home be controlled by the family, and so on. To go into the question on an international scale we might also add that utilities mutually necessary to all the nations be owned by the nations, as the Panama Canal, for instance.—Higgins.

Prince Kropotkin, though not a bolshevik, says approvingly of the Russian revolution that it is trying to build up a society where the whole produce of the joint efforts of labor by technical skill and scientific knowledge should go entirely to the commonwealth; and he declares that for the unavoidable reconstruction of society, by pacific or any other revolutionary means, there must be a union of all the trade unions of the world to free the production of the world from its present enslavement to capitalism.

Higgins and Kropotkin have here put co-operative socialism or communism in a nutshell both as to its aim and program.

The law of self-preservation is ever the same, but whether its salvation is for a part of the people by competition—capitalist salvation, or for the whole people by co-operation—socialist salvation, depends upon whether it rides or is ridden.

So long as the law of self-preservation was supposed to be the will of a conscious, personal god whose earthly representatives were kings and priests or presidents and preachers, the law did the riding within the large domain of animal competition—the domain of capitalism. War is the normal, indeed necessary evil of this domain, and hence the world must have wars so long as it remains within it, and it will remain there so long as it has [Pg 120] celestial divinities with terrestrial representatives in states and churches for its governors.

Now that the law is known to be a matter-force necessity, not a divine decree, the time may rationally be hoped for when the people will do the riding within the small domain of human co-operation—the domain of socialism. Peace is the normal, indeed necessary, state of this domain, and hence the world must cease to have war when it enters it, and is governed by itself instead of by a god and the powers of state and church alleged to have been ordained by him.

Capital punishment should not be administered, if at all, except to a murderer whose guilt has been established to the satisfaction of the great majority of the people in the community to which he belongs, and never in the case of a suspected murderer of whom this is not true.

If William II were really the devil behind the European war by which many millions of the young men of the world have lost their lives, and if Thomas Mooney were really the devil behind the San Francisco explosion by which ten citizens of California lost their lives, their punishment by death might be urged with much show of reason as a social necessity. But if both were hung on the same gallows the world would go on suffering by the ever recurring and closely related misfortunes of war and riot as if nothing had happened. The real devil behind all wars and riots is the capitalist system. There will never be an end of wars and riots until this devil is overthrown.

The so-called Kaiser-war and the so-called Mooney riot are on the same footing, both having the character of an insurrection and both having the aim of self-preservation. The insurrection of the Kaiser was a riot [Pg 121] on behalf of the capitalist class of Germany and for the purpose of protecting it against the capitalist class of England. The insurrection of Mooney (assuming his guilt, merely for illustration) was a riot on behalf of the labor class of California and for the purpose of protecting it against the capitalist class of that state.

Incidentally, both riots have secondary aims of world-wide extent. The Kaiser had two of these: to overthrow the commercial supremacy of England that Germany might have it, and to overthrow industrial republicanism (socialism) everywhere. Mooney had this: the overthrow of commercial imperialism (capitalism) everywhere.

As rioters, there is this in common between Kaiser William and Thomas Mooney, that though moving in opposite directions, they are nevertheless carried by the same matter-force law which manifests itself in the same riotous system, capitalism—a system which, under one form or another, has ever produced international wars and class revolutions; and, so long as it is allowed to exist, never will cease the production of them.

Hence the interests of the world require not that these rioters, Kaiser William and Thomas Mooney, should be hung, but that the capitalist system, which by the operation of the law of self-preservation by animal competitions, produced both of the riots with which they are respectively credited, should be overthrown by the labor system, which, by the operation of the same law of self-preservation by human co-operation, will put an end to all bloody conflicts.

But taking the popular view concerning the responsibility for this commercial war and labor riot and assuming that they should be charged respectively to [Pg 122] Kaiser William and Thomas Mooney, why should the promoter of the little riot die, or worse, suffer imprisonment during life, and the promoter of the big war live?

Yet, if the Kaiser were captured even by England there is no probability that he would be turned over to a court constituted of representatives of the allied nations, tried, found guilty and put to death. Why not? Because, like all wars, his war, no matter which side won the victory, has been upon the whole, or will be in the long run, in the interest of the capitalists of every nation on both sides, at least of the great ones.

If Kaiser William would not be sent to the gallows by such a court why should the court which tried Thomas Mooney be allowed to send him to it; and, especially why, since California is part of a republic, and the Kaiser's war was on behalf of imperialism and a small minority, while Mooney's riot was on behalf of republicanism and the overwhelming majority?

Just now the human part of the world is especially afflicted by unnecessary and therefore unjustifiable deaths. The Governor of California has the opportunity to prevent one such death. I say to him, do it. In the name of Justice and in the name of Humanity, I with millions of others solemnly call upon him to save Mooney, the revolutionist, as Pilate, the Governor of Judea, according to the verdict of all right-thinking men and women, should have saved Jesus, the revolutionist.

III.

You say in effect that we must postulate a divine consciousness to account for human consciousness; but, on [Pg 123] your theory, how could human consciousness come out of a divine consciousness; and, anyhow, contrary to your implication, we know of no consciousness which has come, except by inheritance, from another consciousness, but only of consciousnesses which have come from unconsciousnesses.

Your contention, in this connection, is to the effect that nothing can come out of nothing, and this is the core of a book, "A Short Apology for Being a Christian in the Twentieth Century," by the learned ex-president of Trinity College, Hartford, Dr. Williamson Smith, with whom you have had, I think, some correspondence.

This Apology was written against a letter of mine to the House of Bishops, entitled, "A Natural Gospel for a Scientific Age," which has never seen the light, partly because the ex-President convinced me that if I must give up the orthodox conception of God, I could not hold to the one which I had worked out in the letter.

If you have not seen the ex-President's book, you will, I am sure, enjoy it more than I did, but I doubt whether you will profit as much by it, for it verges towards your lines and away from mine; and so it set me to studying as it will not you, with the result of rejecting the new conception of God which I had worked out for myself, but with it I threw over the old one and ceased to believe in the existence of a conscious, personal divinity. Of course, my faith in the existence of a spiritual world and hope for a future life in it went with the god.

Dr. Williamson Smith and you are entirely correct in the contention that something cannot come out of nothing: but I no longer pretend that it can and I now [Pg 124] see that the stones which have been thrown at me by you both and others have come from glass houses; for this is really the pretension of orthodox theologians. They affirm that the universe was created by God out of nothing, but produce no scrap of evidence for His existence, and even if they could prove that He exists, they would have to admit that He came out of nothing, or at least from something which did so.

It is indeed true that I am unable to tell what matter, force and motion came from, or if I agree with most physicists that they arose from ether, I cannot give its derivative; but, granting that I am as incapable of proving their existence as you are of proving the existence of the Christian trinity, nevertheless I have this immense advantage over you, that I can prove that everything both physical and psychical (including man and his civilization) entering into the constitution of the universe, lives, moves and has its being in my divine trinity—matter, force and motion: whereas you cannot prove that anything is indebted for what it is to your divine trinity—Father, Son and Spirit: therefore I insist that your trinity is a symbol of mine.

What is true of the Christian trinity is true of all the divinities of the supernaturalistic interpretations of religion. The Jews live with no reference to the Christian God, or at least not with any to his second and third persons, and neither Christians nor Jews do so in the case of either the Mohammedan or Buddhistic divinity, and so on, all around the whole circle of gods.

But no representative of any god lives without constant reference to mine, of which yours and all the [Pg 125] others are, as I think, symbols, if they are anything better than fetishes.

If you and ex-President Smith mean by your fundamental thesis, that a thing which is essentially different from that from which it came is an impossibility, you are certainly wrong, for the world is full of such things. In the tree of life there are millions of examples, since (using language in its general significance) everything above the amoeba must be regarded as essentially different from it, though all, including man, came out of it.

Going back as far as we safely can on solid ground, we come to the nebulae from which the solar systems of the universe have evolved, and surely a solar system is as essentially different from the nebula as a man is from an amoeba. Coming to our earth when its primeval, flaming, swirling gases had been condensed into inorganic matter, the protoplasm which is organic matter, arose from it, and so something which grows from within out, comes from something which grows from without in.

The large hoofed horse came from a small five-toed animal, not much larger than a rabbit. The piano and the gun are brother and sister, born of the bow and arrow, yet how different the children from the parent.

An infant is unconscious at birth and what it has of consciousness as a child and an adult is dependent upon the development of its body.

Moreover, as the human body is a development through animal bodies, we may logically conclude that human consciousness is ultimately dependent upon [Pg 126] and inherited from animal consciousness rather than a divine one.

Jesus is represented as saying that God is a spirit; and the fathers of the English part of the Christian reformation said that there is but one living and true God without body, parts or passions. This is their explanation of his conception of God.

When the Jesuine definition of God and the Anglican explanation of it were framed, the Divine Spirit was supposed to be an objective personality.

Modern psychology teaches that no spirit, divine, human or otherwise, is a personality. According to this science, spirit and soul are synonyms for the subjective content of a conscious life, which content consists of feelings, aspirations, ideals, convictions and determinations.

Psychologists know of no spirit or soul without a body constituted of parts any more than physicists know of a force without matter constituted of molecules, atoms, electrons and ions.

Gods represent the religious ideals of people and are symbols of what they think they should be as religionists. They are symbolic, emblematic, parabolic, allegoric devices of the imagination, and contain nothing but the ideal, imaginary things which are put into them by people for themselves, and they do nothing except what the people perform through them in their names for themselves.

Matter and force constitute a machine, an automatic one, which produces things, everything which enters into the constitution of the cosmos, by evolutionary processes, or rather all such things, and there are no [Pg 127] others, are the result of one universal and eternal process of evolution.

What is known as nature is the aggregation of the products of this machine by this process. The machine is unconscious and its workings are mechanical, yet some of its products rise into self-consciousness with the power of self-determination, but both the consciousness and the determination are limited. The infinite consciousness, personality and determination which are postulated of gods are contradictions.

Of all beings man possesses most of consciousness, personality and determination. What he has of these is not dependent upon gods, but all they have of them is dependent upon him. Divine beings are, as to their self-consciousness, personality and determination, human beings personified and placed in the sky. Man does everything for gods. They do nothing for him.

Such are the facts and arguments based upon them, which have forced me step by step over the long way from the position of supernaturalistic traditionalism in its Christian form, still occupied by you, to that of naturalistic scientism in its socialist form which I am now occupying, as tentatively as possible, pending further study in the light of additional facts, for which (some six years ago, when I was desperately battling to prevent the shipwreck of my faith in the god and heaven of orthodox Christianity) I appealed to about 800 outstanding theologians, among them yourself, representing all parts of christendom and every great church, including of course all our bishops among the theologians, and the Anglican communion among the churches.

You may remember how much of correspondence [Pg 128] we had at that time, though neither you nor any one who kindly tried to reach me with the rope of the new scientific apologetics for which I appealed, can realize how eagerly I looked for the replies to my questions, nor the sickness of heart which I experienced when I saw that, in spite of every possible effort of my own and help of others, I was slowly but surely drifting towards what I then thought to be the fatal whirlpools and rocks, but what I now regard as a sheltered port—the golden gate of that delectable country, Marxian socialism, the only heaven that I am now hoping to behold.

You earnestly contend that I am wrong in representing that the majority of outstanding men of science and scientific philosophers do not believe in the existence of a conscious, personal divinity, who created, sustains and governs the universe, or in a conscious, personal life for man beyond the grave, and that none among such scientists and philosophers are orthodox Christians.

Prof. Leuba, the Bryn Mawr psychologist, is one among my authorities for these representations. In his "Belief in God and Immortality" (1916) he exhibits the results of a recent and thorough-going investigation in a chart from which it appears that, taking the greater and lesser representatives of the scientists together, they fall below 50 per cent as to their belief in God, and below 55 per cent in their belief in immortality. [I]

The showing for the scientists who are especially concerned with the origin and destiny of life, biologists and psychologists, is much less favorable [Pg 129] to you; for, taking the greater and lesser together, only 31 per cent of the biologists believe in God and 35 per cent in immortality; and only 25 per cent of the psychologists believe in God, and 20 per cent in immortality.

But the worst by far, is yet to come; for, taking the greater biologists and psychologists, those who count most, of the former 18 per cent believe in God, and 25 per cent in immortality; and of the latter, the greatest of all authorities, only 13 per cent believe in God, and only 8 per cent in immortality.

The greater psychologists are comparatively consistent in that fewer among them believe in a conscious, personal life for humanity beyond the grave than in the conscious, personal life of divinity beyond the clouds. Human immortality is an absurdity without divine existence. The overwhelming majority of great psychologists (the greatest of all authorities, as to whether or not gods "without bodies, parts or passions" can consciously exist in the skies, and disembodied men, women and children in celestial paradises) see this and limit the career of man to earth. In their judgment his heaven and hell are here, and the gods who make and the devils who unmake civilizations are humans, not good or bad divinities.

This is the conclusion of a rapidly increasing number of educated people. A century ago only a few men of science and scientific philosophers had reached it, not twenty five per cent, but now the percentage is nearly ninety and it will soon be ninety-nine. The time is coming, and in the not distant future, when no educated man shall look to the god of any supernaturalistic interpretation of religion for light or [Pg 130] strength, and when none shall hope for a heaven above the earth or fear a hell below it.

> Heav'n but the Vision of fulfill'd Desire, And Hell the Shadow from a Soul on fire Cast on the Darkness into which Ourselves, So late emerg'd from, shall so soon expire.
> —Omar.

Joseph McCabe and Chapman Cohen are among the most brilliant of present day writers on scientific and philosophic subjects. They are not socialists, but both see that modern socialism and orthodox Christianism are utterly irreconcilable incompatibilities.

"How is it that on the Continent democratic bodies are so sceptical, or sceptical bodies so democratic? Precisely because they doubt (or reject altogether) the Christian heaven. They want to make this earth as happy as it can be, to make sure of happiness somewhere. Having taken their eyes from the sky, they have discovered remarkable possibilities in the earth. Having to give less time to God, they have more time to give to man. They think less about their heavenly home, and more about their earthly home. The earthly home has grown very much brighter for the change. The heavenly home is just where it was.

"The plain truth is, of course, that the sentiment which used to be absorbed in religion is now embodied in humanitarianism. Religion is slowly dying everywhere. Social idealism is growing everywhere. People who want to persuade us that social idealism depends on religion are puzzled by this. It is only because they are obstinately determined to connect everything with Christianity, in spite of its historical record. There is no puzzle. We have transferred [Pg 131] our emotions from God to man, from heaven to earth."—Joseph McCabe.

"Socialists who have one eye on the ballot box may assure these people that Socialism is not Atheistic, but few will be convinced. The statement that Socialism has nothing to do with religion, or that many professedly religious people are Socialist, is quite futile. A thoughtful religionist would reply that the first point concedes the truth of all that has been said against Socialism, while the second evades the question at issue. No one is specially concerned with the mental idiosyncracies of individual Socialists; what is at issue is the question whether Socialism does or does not take an Atheistic view of life? He might add, too, that a Socialism which leaves out the belief in God and a future life, which does not, in even the remotest manner, imply these beliefs, which does not make their acceptance the condition of holding the meanest office in the State, and, at most, will merely allow religious beliefs to exist so long as they do not threaten the well-being of the State, is, to all intents and purposes, an Atheistical system."—Chapman Cohen.

In summing up the results of his investigations Prof. Leuba observes that:

In every class of persons investigated, the number of believers in God is less and in most classes very much less than the number of non-believers, and that the number of believers in immortality is somewhat larger than in a personal God; that among the more distinguished, unbelief is very much more frequent than among the less distinguished; and finally that not only the degree of ability, but also the kind of knowledge possessed, is significantly related to the rejection of these beliefs.

In another connection Prof. Leuba speaking of Christian dogmatism as a whole says: [Pg 132]

Christianity, as a system of belief, has utterly broken down, and nothing definite, adequate, and convincing has taken its place. There is no generally acknowledged authority; each one believes as he can, and few seem disturbed at being unable to hold the tenets of the churches. This sense of freedom is the glorious side of an otherwise dangerous situation.

Your conception of the origin, sustenance and governance of the universe is burdened, as are all interpretations of religion which are hinged upon the existence of conscious, personal divinities, with two difficulties: (1) its physical impossibility, and (2) its moral impossibility.

1. Physical Impossibilities. The atomic and molecular movements required for the thinking of a single man would be beyond the capacity of all the gods of the supernaturalistic interpretations of religion together.

Some idea of the number of such motions which are taking place in every human brain, will be derived from the conservative representations of Hofmeister as exhibited in the following condensed form by McCabe in his book, "The Evolution of Mind:"

We have reason to believe that there are in each molecule of ordinary protoplasm at least 450 atoms of carbon, 720 atoms of hydrogen, 116 of nitrogen, 6 of sulphur, and 140 of oxygen. Nerve-plasm is still more complex.

Recent discoveries have only increased the wonder and potentiality of the cortex. Each atom has proved to be a remarkable constellation of electrons, a colossal reservoir of energy. The atom of hydrogen contains about 1,000 electrons, the atom of carbon 12,000, the atom of nitrogen 14,000, the atom of oxygen 16,000, and the atom of sulphur 32,000. These electrons [Pg 133] circulate within the infinitesimal space of the atom at a speed of from 10,000 to 90,000 miles a second. It would take 340,000 barrels of powder to impart to a bullet the speed with which some of these particles dart out of their groups. A gramme of hydrogen—a very tiny portion of the simplest gas—contains energy enough to lift a million tons more than a hundred yards.

Of these astounding arsenals of energy, the atoms, we have, on the lowest computation, at least 600 million billion in the cortex of the human brain.

Scientists, says Professor Olerich, in his book, "A Modern Look at the Universe," estimate that the chemical atom is so infinitesimally small that it requires a group of not less than a billion to make the group barely visible under the most powerful microscope, and a thousand such groups would have to be put together in order to make it just visible to the naked eye as a mere speck floating in the sunbeam.

The microscope reveals innumerable animalcules in the hundredth part of a drop of water. They all eat, digest, move and from all appearances of their frolics, they are endowed with sensation and ability of enjoyment. What then shall we say of the minuteness of the food they eat; of the blood that surges through their veins; of their nervous system that thrills and guides them? Their minutest organs must be composed of molecules, atoms, ions and electrons inconceivably smaller than are the organs themselves.

Is there any god in a celestial field who could care for the movements which occur in the molecules constituting a hundredth part of a drop of water, not to speak of those which occur in the bodies of its myriads of inhabitants? And what shall we say of all the inorganic and organic movements in a small cup of whole drops of water, let alone those of a great ocean of them? [Pg 134]

But why go further into this subject? Is not the utter childishness of the orthodox representative of a supernaturalistic interpretation of religion, who credits his god with the governance of the motions occurring in the mineral, vegetable and animal kingdoms of this globe, leaving out of account those of its solar system, and of other systems which constitute the universe, sufficiently manifest?

If you say that the motions which issue in the phenomena of the universe are regulated by a law which was once for all willed by the god of the Christian interpretation of religion, I ask why the law should be credited to the willing of this god rather than to that of the god of Jewish, Mohammedan or Buddhistic interpretation.

Newton took the first of the six initiatory steps in the long way which led to the conclusion that the universe is self-existing, self-sustaining and self-governing, by showing that all the movements of the solar systems were necessarily what they have been by reason of a matter-force law, gravitation. This discovery is the most momentous event in the whole history of mankind.

Laplace took the second step by showing that the cosmic nebulae contain within themselves all the potentialities necessary to the formation of solar systems.

Lavoisier took the third step by showing that the matter which enters into the constitution of the universe is an eternality.

Mayer took the fourth step by showing that the force which enters into the constitution of the universe is an eternality. [Pg 135]

Darwin took the fifth step by showing that the protoplasm contains all the potentialities of every form of physical and degree of psychical life from the moneron to man; that all representatives of both the vegetable and animal kingdoms, including man, are related and so on a level as to their origin and destiny, and that the different species are the natural results of the necessary struggle with rivals and with adverse environments for existence.

Marx took the sixth step by showing that the essential difference between humans and beasts is primarily a question of the hand and secondarily of the machines by which its efficiency is immeasurably increased; that slavery has been and must continue to be the means of advancement towards the ideal civilization; that the kinds of human slavery were what they have been because machines have been what they were, and that the time is coming when the slaves will no longer be men, women and children, but machines which will be exploited for the good of the many, not the profit of the few—then, and not until then, rapid advance shall be made towards the goal where the whole world shall be one great co-operative family, every member of which shall have the greatest of possible opportunities to make the most of terrestrial life by having it as long and happy as possible.

2. Moral Impossibilities. The moral impossibility of the assumptions of these apologies is seen by all who have eyes for seeing things as they are in the fact that if God is credited with the good He must also be debited with the evil. If for example, He endowed the human body with its useful and necessary [Pg 136] parts. He also endowed it with its harmful and unnecessary parts.

Experts in the field of anatomy tell us that there are in our bodies at least 180 useless parts, some among which are the occasion of much suffering and many premature deaths, the vermiform appendix alone causing many thousands of such cases annually.

Do you not see that these useless structures, all of which are inherited from the lower animals, are so many evidences of the truth of Darwinism and the untruthfulness of Mosaism? Eleven of these wholly useless and more or less harmful inheritances have been of no use to any of our ancestors from the fish up and four are inherited from our reptilian and amphibian forefathers, but according to Moses we have no such progenitors.

Admitting the fact of the existence of evil there is no escaping from the logical conclusions of dear, old sensible Epicurus:

Either God is willing to remove evil from this world and cannot, or he can and is not willing, or finally he can and is willing. If he is willing and cannot, it is impotence, which is contrary to the nature of God. If he can and is unwilling, it is wickedness, and that is no less contrary to the nature of God. If he is not willing and cannot, there is both wickedness and impotence. If he is willing and can, which is the only one of these suppositions that can be applied to God, how happens it that there is evil on earth?

Oh, if only the world had been influenced by this logic instead of by the metaphysics of the supernaturalistic interpretations of religion, it would have been so far on the way towards the ideal civilization as to have long since passed the point where it would [Pg 137] have been possible to have the world war which has recently deluged the earth with blood and tears, or to make the Versailles treaty which is destined to issue in one war after another, ever filling the world fuller with the tyranny, poverty, slavery and misery which are the inevitable concomitants of all wars.

In my opinion the fascinating essayist, Mallock, has written the best of all apologies for theism. I cannot imagine a better one. He, however, makes no more attempt than Sir Oliver Lodge does to establish Christianity, or any other supernaturalistic interpretations of religion. Like Kant and yourself, Mallock takes his stand on the ground that a belief in a celestial God, and in the immortality which goes with it, is necessary to morality, the basic virtue upon which civilization rests. As Kant admits that the existence of God cannot be inferred from pure reason, so Mallock admits and even strongly contends that it cannot be established on scientific grounds. I quote a striking passage:

> We must divest ourselves of all foregone conclusions, of all question-begging reverences, and look the facts of the universe steadily in the face.
>
> If theists will but do this, what they will see will astonish them. They will see that if there is anything at the back of this vast process, with a consciousness and a purpose in any way resembling our own—a Being who knows what he wants and is doing his best to get it—he is, instead of a holy and all-wise God, a scatter-brained, semi-powerful, semi-impotent monster. They will recognize as clearly as they ever did the old familiar facts which seemed to them evidences of God's wisdom, love and goodness; but they will find that these facts, when taken in connection with the others, only supply us with a stan [Pg 138] dard in the nature of this being himself by which most of his acts are exhibited to us as those of a criminal madman. If he had been blind, he had not had sin; but if we maintain that he can see, then his sin remains. Habitually a bungler as he is, and callous when not actively cruel, we are forced to regard him, when he seems to exhibit benevolence, as not divinely benevolent, but merely weak and capricious, like a boy who fondles a kitten and the next moment sets a dog at it. And not only does his moral character fall from him bit by bit, but his dignity disappears also. The orderly processes of the stars and the larger phenomena of nature are suggestive of nothing so much as a wearisome court ceremonial surrounding a king who is unable to understand or to break away from it; whilst the thunder and whirlwind, which have from time immemorial been accepted as special revelations of his awful power and majesty, suggest, if they suggest anything of a personal character at all, merely some blackguardly larrikin kicking his heels in the clouds, not perhaps bent on mischief, but indifferent to the fact that he is causing it.
>
> But we need not attempt to fill in the picture further. The truth is, as we consider the universe as a whole, it fails to suggest a conscious and purposive God at all; and it fails to do so not because the processes of evolution as such preclude the idea that God might have made use of them for a definite purpose, but because when we

come to consider these processes in detail, and view them in the light of the only purposes they suggest, we find them to be such that a God who could deliberately have been guilty of them would be a God too absurd, too monstrous, too mad to be credible.

The god who had any part in bringing upon the world the English-German war, the Versailles peace, the Russian blockade, is for me a devil not a divinity. [Pg 139] If you say that the Christian god had nothing to do with them, I reply that these are among the greatest of all curses wherewith mankind has been afflicted in modern times; and if he could not or would not prevent them, what ground is there for looking to him for help in any time of need?

How can I adequately express my contempt for the assertion that all things occur for the best, for a wise and beneficent end? It is the most utter falsehood, and a crime against the human race.... Human suffering is so great, so endless, so awful, that I can hardly write of it.... The whole and the worst, the worst pessimist can say is far beneath the least particle of the truth.... Anyone who will consider the affairs of the world at large ... will see that they do not proceed in the manner they would do for our happiness if a man of humane breadth of view were placed at their head with unlimited power. A man of intellect and humanity could cause everything to happen in an infinitely superior manner. But that which is ... credited to a non-existent intelligence (or cosmic "order," it is just the same) should really be claimed and exercised by the human race. We must do for ourselves what superstition has hitherto supposed an intelligence to do for us.—Richard Jeffries.

> Would but some winged Angel ere too late Arrest the yet unfolded Roll of Fate, And make the stern Recorder otherwise Enregister, or quite obliterate!
> Ah Love! could you and I with Him conspire To grasp this sorry Scheme of Things entire, Would not we shatter it to bits—and then Remold it nearer to the Heart's Desire!
> —Omar.

[Pg 140]

You frequently intimate that my doctrine concerning the origin and destiny of the universe with all that therein is, including man, is not that of the majority of men of science and scientific philosophers, but that yours is. It will therefore be of interest to you to know that I have submitted the most radical of my materialistic pieces to three men of science, all great authorities, one of whom replied, that he was in substantial agreement with me, but thought me to be 400 years ahead of our time; another, that he found nothing to criticize unless it might be my failure to give greater prominence to the fact that the gods of the redemptive interpretations, of religion were so many versions of the sun-myth, and the other, that the essay would pass any world congress of scientists by a large majority.

You think that I am wrong in quoting Newton and Darwin on my side, because they believed in the existence of a conscious, personal god. I am persuaded that such was not the case with Darwin at his death; but, however this may be, it is in neither of these cases, nor in that of any other scientist, a question of what he philosophically believed concerning a god, but of what he scientifically established as a fact.

Newton established the fact that the movements of the stars in their courses are naturally regulated by the law of gravitation, not supernaturally by the will of a god.

Darwin established the fact that all living species of animal and vegetable life exist as the natural results of evolutionary processes, not as the supernatural results of creative acts.

If Newton were to stand by his theological writ [Pg 141] ings, he would fall in your estimation, for his work on the book of Daniel would be regarded by you as an absurdity. He considered Daniel to be the great revelation of a God, Jehovah, but you know it to be the purest fiction of a man, quite as much the work of the imagination of its author as Don Quixote is that of Cervantes.

Among the many theological authorities whom you quote against me, the greatest, in my estimation, is Dr. Inge, Dean of St. Paul's, London, whose utterances I have been noting with great interest of late; partly, no doubt, because he seems to be giving up your orthodox side and coming over, slowly but surely, to my heterodox one.

In a London paper which has just reached me, the Literary Guide, this is said of the Dean:

The theological opinions of Dean Inge, one of the official mouthpieces of the Church of England, and probably the most distinguished spokesman for the more liberally minded of the clergy, have now reached an interesting stage, both for those without the Church as well as for those within it. Although he does not feel called upon to state his own private conclusions on such debatable questions, he no longer regards the doctrines of the Immaculate Conception and the Bodily Resurrection as essential prerequisites of Christianity and would consider fit for ordination any candidate who rejected them, provided such a person still acknowledged the divine nature of Jesus Christ—that is, he would not exclude him from the Church's ministry.

If I understand Dean Inge as he is reported in the article of which this is the opening paragraph, he bases his faith in the divinity of Jesus upon the uniqueness of his character and teachings, not on the miraculousness of his birth and healings. [Pg 142]

But Dean Inge has no authentic or reliable account of the life and teachings of Jesus; and so, as a theologian, like all theologians, he lives, moves and has his being in the realm of fiction, the difference between him and yourself being that he is in that part of it where the imagination sits enthroned, and you in the region where metaphysics is monarch of all it surveys.

An outstanding theologian who, as it seems to me, overshadows Dean Inge, commenting upon a piece of my writing which is quite as radical as any part of this letter goes even further than he.

"I have," he says, "just read the Chapter of your Natural Gospel for a Scientific Age, which you have kindly sent me, with the greatest interest. Indeed I have come so heartily to share your point of view that I can find no points for criticism; I can only say how grateful I am to have had an opportunity of seeing your uncompromising and clear expression of the only kind of Modernism that has any promise for the future. I am beginning to feel more and more uncomfortable in our Christian movement because so many of our leaders here are attempting an impossible compromise with dogma. Men like Dr. Rashdall have no place in the movement for men who cannot accept their 'fullblooded theism.' In fact they are Harnackians with their one or two unalterably fixed dogmas."

IV.

If you ask why I continue to be a member of an orthodox church and its ministry, the answer is, there is no reason why I should not for (if they may be interpreted by myself, for myself, spiritually) I accept every article of the creed of catholic orthodoxy; but if the articles of this creed must be interpreted lit [Pg 143] erally there is no one in our church (the Episcopal) or in any among the churches, who believes all of them. For example, who believes, that God created the heavens and the earth out of nothing in six days, as he is represented to have done in his alleged revelation of which the creed is a condensation? All in this church, or at least all the ministers of it, who have obeyed its requirement respecting the devotion of themselves to study, as I have, know that the firmament or heaven of which the revelation speaks has no substantial existence, only an imaginary one. What was supposed to be it, is but the reflection of light upon the dust of the atmosphere. As for the earth it was not made out of nothing; and, indeed, it was not supernaturally made at all but naturally evolutionized out of matter and force, and even they were not created by a god, for they are co-existing eternalities; nor were their evolutionary processes directed by him, for they have eternally, automatically and necessarily co-operated in such processes to the production of every phenomenon which has contributed to make both the physical and psychical parts of the universe what they have been at any time, including the divine, diabolical and angelic fictions which men have made and placed above and below the earth.

If you ask whether I am still a professing Christian, I will answer: yes, yet the Brother Jesus of the New Testament, catholic creed and protestant confessions, is not for me an historical personage, but only a symbol of all that is for the good of the world, even as the Uncle Sam of American literature is not an historical personage but only a symbol of all which is for the good of the United States. [Pg 144]

If you ask whether I am a praying Christian, I shall answer: yes, yet when I pray, as I do every day, my prayer is an appeal to a real divinity within my heart, the better self, of which self all the unreal divinities in the skies including the Christian trinity, Father, Son and Spirit, are but poetic symbols, and I no longer expect this God to answer otherwise than the symbol of parents, Santa Claus, answers the prayers of children, or the symbol of the United States, Uncle Sam, answers the prayers of Americans.

If you ask whether I am a communing Christian, I shall answer: yes, yet when I go to the Lord's Supper, as I do every month, the strength which I receive is derived from the feeling that through it I place myself in communion with my human brethren on earth, not with a divine brother in the sky, particularly with the members of my church and the citizens of my town and its neighborhood, but generally with all men, women and children throughout the whole world, of which real brethren the brother god in the sky, Jesus, is but a poetic symbol; nor do I now regard the communion of this supper as being essentially different from that of any ordinary family-meal, lodge-banquet, or socialist-picnic, with each of which repasts the informal Lord's Supper of the apostolic church had much more in common than it has with the formal celebrations of the sacrament in any among the sectarian churches. [J]

Many critics represent that, in view of the changes in my theological opinion, if I am an honest man, not [Pg 145] a hypocrite, I will leave the ministry and communion of the Episcopal Church. But why should I go while any of my brother clergymen remain? I give a symbolic or allegorical interpretation to every article of the whole system of Christian supernaturalism and uniqueism; yet as symbols, allegories, parables, or myths, I do not reject any, and no member of our House of Bishops literally accepts all.

Who among influential preachers of any rank in any church believes: (1) that the world was made about six thousand years ago by a personal, Creator-God out of nothing; or that it was made at any time out of anything? (2) that such a God formed Adam out of dust and Eve out of a rib; that they left His hands as perfect physical and moral images of Himself, and fully civilized representatives of the human race; or that there was any first man and woman? (3) that He planted a Garden of Eden and placed them therein under ideal conditions, and that He walked in it and talked with them; or that there ever was any such garden? (4) that a personal destroyer-Devil, incarnated in a talking serpent, tempted them into disobedience; or that there ever was any such Devil? (5) that but for this Devil's influence and their sin, labor and suffering, physical death and moral degradation would have been unknown on earth, and that it would have been the permanent abode of mankind, as indeed of all sentient creatures; or that any of the higher forms of life would have been possible without death? and (6) that to repair the evils accomplished by this Destroyer-Devil it was necessary for a personal Restorer-God to become incarnated in a man, in order that he might shed this blood as a sufficient sacrifice for the satisfaction of the offended [Pg 146] Creator-God; also, in order that the resurrection of the bodies (bones, flesh, blood and animal organism) of all deceased men, women and children and the rehabitation of them by their respective souls could be accomplished, to the end that a few, on account of their faith, might be transferred to a permanent home in a heaven on a firmament above the earth, and the many, because of their lack of faith, to a permanent home in a hell below; or that there ever was any such incarnation for these purposes; or that there are any such firmament, heaven, and hell, or that there will be any such resurrection, ascension or descension?

If other bishops, priests and deacons can, as they must, bring in their symbolism or allegorism touching any or all of these six fundamentals, which constitute the basis of the supernaturalism of traditional Christianity, and yet not leave the church, why may not I bring in mine and remain?

Attention is called by several critics to Sir Oliver Lodge, as an example of an outstanding man of science who accepts supernaturalism. While I was desperately trying to retain my conception of a supernaturalistic God and of all the supernaturalism that goes with it (revelation of truth, answer to prayer, guidance by providence, resurrection of the dead and their ascension, eternal consciousness and happiness) I at one time centered a great deal of hope in him, and eagerly studied his works as indeed I did those of most apologists for supernaturalism among them the greatest, Flammarion, Balfour, Bergson and Hudson, but my careful study of his many writings convinced me that he does not hold any of the supernaturalistic doctrines which are distinctively Christian.

However, it is my doctrine concerning Jesus, rather [Pg 147] than that of Christian traditionalism, that is in exact alignment with that of this renowned physicist. We agree that Jesus, if historical, was a Son of God and the Christ to men in no other sense, and therefore in no higher degree, than all representatives of the human race may be sons or daughters of God, if there are gods and christs, to the men, women and children with whom they come in contact.

Most critics think that I am wrong in representing that the great majority of the leading men of science are naturalistic, not supernaturalistic, but Sir Oliver Lodge represents that among such scientists it is generally believed that the universe is "self-explained, self-contained and self-maintained;" and speaking on his own behalf of its creation out of nothing he says: "The improbability or absurdity of such a conception, except in the symbolism of poetry, is extreme, and it is unthinkable by any educated person."

All these gods were created, endowed and located by man, and then he had them make revelations, create churches, institute sacraments and appoint priesthoods for his redemption from devils whom he also created, endowed and located.

This is why people of the same country and time have such different gods and revelations. Jehovah is the god and the Old Testament the revelation of the kings and plutocrats who are responsible for wars; Jesus is the god and the New Testament is the revelation of the doctors and nurses who do what they can to alleviate the misery of them.

The gods, not excepting Jehovah and Jesus, are as mythical as Santa Claus and answer their suppliants not otherwise than he answers his, through human representatives. If the suffering, needy or afflicted do [Pg 148] not get help and sympathy from men, women and children they get none from the gods and angels.

While on the one hand the great majority of scientists, scientific philosophers and educated people generally doubt that any god ever answered a prayer or exercised a providence, on the other, no one doubts that men, women and children answer millions of prayers daily and that every person's career is wholly different from what it would have been but for human providence; that, indeed, life would be impossible without the providence which all people exercise in the hearing and answering of prayers.

Representatives of many of the interpretations of religion strewed every battle-field of the European war. The celestial saviours did not care for one of their devotees. The terrestrial saviours (doctors and nurses) did everything for the desperately wounded and saved millions who would have miserably perished but for them. These were the real christs and angels of whom the celestial ones are but symbols. The celestials always have passed by on the other side. The terrestrials are the Good Samaritans when there are any.

Sceptics infer from this negligence that the gods and angels have no real objective existence. Believers contend that they really exist objectively and excuse the neglect on account of preoccupation. For example, the God of traditional Christianity is supposed to spend much time counting hairs on the heads of His people and watching sparrows fall to the ground. Sceptics are reverently but earnestly asking: Why does He not keep the sparrows from falling? Why does He not let the hairs remain unnumbered, until He has put a stop to wars and promoted good will [Pg 149] among men to a degree which will render it impossible that the world should any longer be cursed by them?

If believers say that we have no knowledge of the ways of God, sceptics reply: Since all which is known about any objective reality is concerning the ways thereof, what the action is under given circumstances, how do you know that your God has anything to do with either sparrows or men, or even that He exists?

As to their philosophy concerning the origin, sustenance and governance of the universe, socialists of the school of Marx, are almost to a man materialists; but, as to their philosophy concerning life, they are as generally idealists. There is, I feel sure, as much idealism in my thinking and living now as there was in the days of my orthodoxy, but I will let you judge for yourself after reading the following confession of faith:

My early life was blighted as the result of the premature death of my father by the Civil War and the consequent breaking up of his family and my bondage to a German who made a slave of me, broke my health by overwork and exposure, and, worst of all, kept me in ignorance, so that when, at the age of twenty-one, I began my education, I was assigned to the fourth grade of a public school.

The prime of my life has been wasted in preaching as truths the dogmas of the Christian theology, the representations of which I now believe, with the overwhelming majority of educated people, to be at best so many symbols and at worst superstitions.

But though I do not now and probably never shall again believe in the existence of a conscious, personal god, a knowledge of and obedience to whose will is [Pg 150] necessary to salvation, yet an injustice is done me by those who say I have abandoned god and religion.

Every one who desires and endeavors to fulfill the requirements of a law which is independent of his will and beyond his control has a god and a religion. I desire and endeavor this in the case of two such laws and so have two gods and two religions. Both of my divinities are trinities. One is in the physical realm and the other in the moral one.

In the physical realm my triune god is: matter, the father; force, the son, and motion, the spirit.

In the moral realm, my triune god is: fact, the father; truth, the son, and life, the spirit.

For me the triune divinity of Christianity is a symbol of these trinities and it is my desire and effort to discover and fulfill what they require of me, in order that I may make my own physical, psychical and moral life as long, happy and complete as possible and help others in doing this for themselves. This desire and effort is at once my morality and religion, my politics and patriotism, and they are spiritual realities.

On account of the first of these sets of spiritual virtues (morality and religion) I claim to be a Christian of the highest type, and that any accusation which is raised against me because of alleged disloyalty to any essential of Christianism is an injustice.

On account of the second of these sets of spiritual virtues (politics and patriotism) I claim to be an American of the highest type, and that any accusation which is raised against me because of alleged disloyalty to an essential of Americanism is an injustice.

From the viewpoint of the self-styled one hundred [Pg 151] per cent Christians, I am a betrayer of Brother Jesus because I do not believe that he ever had any existence as a god and that, if he was at any time a man, the world does not now and never can know of one thing that he did or of one word that he said.

From the viewpoint of the self-styled one hundred per cent Americans, I am a traitor to Uncle Sam, because I did oppose his going into the English-German war, and because I do object to the partiality which he shows to his rich nephews and nieces.

Still Jesus and Uncle Sam are as dear to me as ever and indeed dearer, yet not as objective, conscious personalities, but as symbols, ideals or patterns.

However, though I love my Brother Jesus and Uncle Sam all the time, as a child does Santa Claus at Christmas time, I am no longer childish enough at any time to look to either of them to do anything for me, because I know that what is done for me must be done either by myself or by men, women and children, and that as objective, conscious personalities, my Brother Jesus and Uncle Sam have had no more to do with my life than the man-in-the-moon.

Your observation concerning the American government as being the standard to which all governments will ultimately conform challenges an earnest word of friendly dissent.

Our government is what all the governments of the world are (with the single exception of the Russian) a government in the interest of a small class, the representatives of which own the means and machines of production and distribution and who produce and distribute things for profit, each for himself.

The representatives of one class produce things socially, and those of another class appropriate them [Pg 152] individually. This is capitalistic anarchy, the worst of possible anarchism, and it must have an end soon or the world will be lost.

Robbery is the essence of anarchy and Marx showed that every cent of profit made under the existing system of economics (and in the United States it amounts to several billions of dollars every year) is so much robbery of the many who make and operate the machines, because they are paid less in wages than the value of the products made and distributed by them.

We are hearing much in these days about the anarchy of those who are dissatisfied with the capitalistic governments, but the governments themselves and those in whose interests they exist are the real anarchists. The flesh and blood of anarchism are robbery and lying, and these are the meat and drink of capitalism.

The English-German war was the most flagrant act of anarchy in the whole history of mankind. The peace of Versailles and the blockade of Russia were outrageous acts of anarchy, and so also are the terrorism and tyranny of which every capitalistic country is so full, our own with the rest.

Morality is the very heart of civilization and of all that really makes for it; but morality is impossible on a capitalistic basis, for it is founded on the most immoral things in the world, robbery, lying, murder, ignorance, poverty and slavery.

If I am right in the conviction that the United States is more wholly given over to capitalism than any other nation, not excepting even England, it is the greatest robber, liar and murderer on earth. How [Pg 153] then, can the United States become the standard for the governments of the nations?

If the government of Russia holds its own, it, rather than that of the United States, will become the standard to which all governments must measure up or else go down.

Yes, not the government of the United States but that of Russia is destined to become the standard of all peoples, for the aim of our government is money, more money, and then some, for the few, while the infinitely higher aim of theirs is life, more life, fuller life for every man, woman and child.

Within my generation the vanguard of humanity has passed from the age of traditionalism to that of scientism and this transition is the greatest and most salutary event in the whole history of humanity. It is impossible to exaggerate its importance. It marks the time when man began consciously to realize that he must look to himself rather than to any god for salvation.

From time immemorial man has realized that ignorance is his ruin and knowledge his salvation, but during the too many and too long ages of traditionalism he made the fatal mistake of supposing that he was dependent upon a supernatural revelation by an unconscious, personal god for the necessary knowledge. But now the leading people of the world, the shepherds of the sheep, are seeing with increasing clearness that man has naturally inherited his knowledge and must naturally acquire by his own experience, reason and investigation every addition to it.

The world is indeed passing through a long, dark night, but neither the longest nor the darkest, and [Pg 154] since at last a great and rapidly increasing multitude happily realize that humanity must work out its own salvation through the living of its own knowledge by its own inherited and increased strength, not by a supernatural grace, we of this generation may rationally hope, as those of no other did or could, for the dawning of the longest and brightest of all days.

As an old year dies into a new one, and as flourishing generations die into rising ones, so the old traditional ages, when nations and sects looked to their rival gods in the skies for help, are happily dying into the new scientific age, when all sensible and good men, relying upon the strength of a common divinity which is within themselves, will unite in an all-inclusive brotherhood for the promotion of the ideal civilization, a universal reign of righteousness.

It is night,—midnight. The clock is striking twelve. But this is the very hour and the very minute, when all the saviours of mankind have always been and ever will be born. Then it is that the Virgin, Nature, comes to this dark world with her new born Son, Truth, whom to know and follow is morality, religion, politics and life. It is then that those who give expression to the highest ideals and deepest longings of mankind, hear the angels, Reason and Hope, sing: On earth peace and good will towards men.

Very cordially and gratefully yours,
WM. M. BROWN.

Brownella Cottage,
Galion, Ohio.

[Pg 155]

FREDERICK ENGELS

[Pg 156]

NIKOLAI LENIN

FOOTNOTES:

[H] The difference between a political republic, such as America has developed, and an industrial republic, such as Russia is developing, is that the administrators of the former are elected from the geographical divisions and those of the latter from the productive divisions into which the population is divided.

If we liken states to fruit trees, the American tree may be said to have been evolutionized for the purpose of producing the fruit of commodities for the profit of the owning class, and the Russian, the fruit of commodities for the use of the working class.

[I] See appendix.

[J] Nevertheless I consider church-going to be a bad habit, and if I could live my life over, I would not allow myself to become addicted to it.

[Pg 157]

COMMUNISM AND CHRISTIANISM

ANALYZED AND CONTRASTED FROM THE MARXIAN AND DARWINIAN POINTS OF VIEW

Appendix.

Morality is the greatest thing in the world; but paradoxical as it may seem, there is one greater thing, liberty—the liberty which is freedom to learn, interpret, live and teach the truth as it is revealed by the facts or acts of nature. Without this freedom there can be no morality, and of course no true religion, politics or civilization.

[Pg 158]

SURVIVAL OF THE FITTEST.

In northern climes, the polar bear Protects himself with fat and hair, Where snow is deep and ice is stark, And half the year is cold and dark; He still survives a clime like that By growing fur, by growing fat. These traits, O bear, which thou transmittest Prove the Survival of the Fittest.

To polar regions waste and wan, Comes the encroaching race of man, A puny, feeble, little bubber, He has no fur, he has no blubber. The scornful bear sat down at ease To see the stranger starve and freeze; But, lo! the stranger slew the bear, And ate his fat and wore his hair; These deeds, O Man, which thou committest Prove the Survival of the Fittest.

In modern times the millionaire Protects himself as did the bear: Where Poverty and Hunger are He counts his bullion by the car: Where thousands perish still he thrives— The wealth, O Croesus, thou transmittest Proves the Survival of the Fittest.

But, lo, some people odd and funny, Some men without a cent of money— The simple common human race Chose to improve their dwelling place; They had no use for millionaires, They calmly said the world was theirs, They were so wise, so strong, so many, The Millionaires?—there wasn't any. These deeds, O Man, which thou committest Prove the Survival of the Fittest.

—Mrs. Charlotte Stetson.

[Pg 159]

I. SCIENTIFIC SOCIALISM.

The working class and the employing class have nothing in common. There can be no peace so long as hunger and want are found among millions of working people and the few, who make up the employing class, have all the good things of life.

Between these two classes a struggle must go on until the workers of the world organize as a class, take possession of the earth and the machinery of production, and abolish the wage system.

We find that the centering of management of the industries into fewer and fewer hands makes the trade unions unable to cope with the ever growing power of the employing class. The trade unions foster a state of affairs which allows one set of workers to be pitted against another set of workers in the same industry, thereby helping defeat one another in wage wars. Moreover, the trade unions aid the employing class to mislead the workers into the belief that the working class have interests in common with their employers.

These conditions can be changed and the interest of the working class upheld only by an organization formed in such a way that all its members in any one industry, or in all industries if necessary, cease work whenever a strike or lockout is on in any department thereof, thus making an injury to one an injury to all.

Instead of the conservative motto, "A fair day's wage for a fair day's work", we must inscribe on our banner the revolutionary watchword, "Abolition of the wage system".

It is the historic mission of the working class to do away with capitalism. The army of production must be organized, not only for the every-day struggle with capitalists, but also to carry on production when capitalism shall have been overthrown. By organizing industrially we are forming the structure of the new society within the shell of the old. —Preamble of the Industrial Workers of the World.

The following Synopsis of Scientific Socialism will serve both as a summary of and supplement to my little book. It is the introductory part of a catechism (a series of questions and answers) entitled "Scientific Socialism Study Course" published by Charles H. [Pg 160] Kerr & Company, 341 East Ohio Street, Chicago, and is reprinted here by their consent, with certain changes in the interests of brevity and perspicuity. As a whole this short Study Course of only thirty small pages in large type is the greatest piece of catechetical literature of which I have any knowledge. Even the synopsis as given here contains more of the education which makes for the good of the world than all the catechisms of all the churches. The Catechism was published in 1913.

1. How do you explain the phenomena of History?

Ans.: History, from the capitalist point of view, is a record of political and intellectual changes and revolutions of so-called great men, wherein the economic causes for these acts and changes are ignored or concealed; but, from the socialist view point, history reveals a series of class struggles between an exploited wealth-producing class and an exploiting ruling class over the wealth produced.

2. What effect have "great men" had on history?

Ans.: Great men were simply ideal expressions of the hopes of some class in society that was becoming economically powerful. They formed a nucleus around which a class gathered itself in attaining economic conquests in its own interest, and in establishing social institutions in harmony with, and for the perpetuation of, such class interests. These men had to embody some vital principles from the economic conditions of their time and represent some class interest. The same men with the same ideas would not be great men under a different mode of production when the time for their ideas was not ripe.

3. What great factor is responsible for the rise of "great men?"

Ans.: The fact that the ideas of these men coincided with the class interests of some class in society that was becoming economically powerful. Therefore economic conditions must exist or be developing [Pg 161] which find their highest expression in the ideas of such men.

4. Why do social institutions change and not remain fixed?

Ans.: Because the process of economic evolution will not permit them to remain fixed. The development and improvement of the means of production and distribution produce economic changes, therefore social institutions (the state, church, school and even the family) are forced to change to conform with changing economic conditions. These are due to evolutionary and revolutionary processes connected with the means of production and distribution.

5. What is responsible for the birth of new ideas, and do they occur to some one individual only?

Ans.: New ideas, theories and discoveries emanate from material conditions, and such conditions act upon individuals. The same idea or discovery may be brought out by different individuals independently and apart from each other. This proves that it is not great men who are responsible for material conditions, but that material conditions (modes of production and distribution) produce the men best able to marshal the facts and express the idea; usually in the interest of some class.

6. What single great idea occurred to both Darwin and Wallace independently?

Ans.: The theory of "Natural Selection" which showed that the closely allied ante-type was the parent stock from which the new form had been derived by variation.

7. What single great idea occurred to both Marx and Engels independently?

Ans.: The "Materialistic Conception of History."

8. Name the three great ideas developed by Marx and Engels which now form the bed-rock basis for the socialist philosophy.

Ans.: (1) the Materialistic Conception of History, or, the law of economic determinism, (2) the Law of Surplus Value, and (3) the Class Struggle. [Pg 162]

9. Explain, briefly, the "materialistic conception of history."

Ans.: "In every historical epoch, the prevailing mode of economic production and exchange and the social organization necessarily following from it forms the basis upon which is built up and from which alone can be explained, the political and intellectual history of that epoch." The laws, customs, education, religion, public opinion and morals are in the long run controlled and shaped by economic conditions; or, in other words, by the dominant ruling class which the economic system of any given period forces to the front.

10. What is the most important question in life?

Ans.: The problem of securing food and shelter.

11. What bearing does this have on the materialistic conception of history?

Ans.: It gives us the only key by which we can understand the history of the past, and within limits, predict the course of future development.

12. What effect does the prevailing mode of production and exchange in any particular epoch, have on the social organization and political and intellectual history of that epoch?

Ans.: "Anything that goes to the roots of the economic structure and modifies it (the food and shelter question in life) will inevitably modify every other branch and department of human life, political, ethical, religious and moral. This makes the social question primarily an economic one and all our thought and effort should be concentrated on it."

13. Do the ideas of the ruling class, in any given epoch, correspond with the prevailing mode of economic production?

Ans.: They correspond exactly, as all connective institutions, civil, religious, legal, educational, political and domestic have been moulded in the interest of the economically dominant class who control these institutions in a manner to uphold their class interests where their ideas find expression. [Pg 163]

14. What effect do these ideas of the ruling class have on the interests of the subject class?

Ans.: The effect is detrimental to the interests of the subject class as the different class interests conflict. Therefore the ruling class finds the institutions mentioned very useful in either persuading or forcing the so-called "lower classes" to submit to the economic conditions that are absolutely against their interest, even though they are the wealth producing class.

15. Distinguish natural environment from man-made environment.

Ans.: Natural environment which consisted of the fertility of the soil, climatic conditions, abundance of fruits, nuts, game and fish was all-important in the early stage of man's development. With the progress of civilization this nature-made environment loses its supreme importance and the man-made economic environment becomes equally important.

16. Explain, briefly, the law of Surplus Value.

Ans.: It is the difference between what the working class as a whole gets for its labor power at its value in wages, say an average of five dollars per day, for producing commodities, and what the employing class as a whole gets, say an average of twenty-five dollars, for the same commodities when sold at their value. According to this conservative estimate capital is upon the whole and in the long run robbing labor of four-fifths of the value of its productive power. Capitalism is therefore the great robber, the Beelzebub of robbers.

17. Since the economic factor is the determining factor, what does the law of Surplus Value furnish us?

Ans.: "Surplus Value is the key to the whole present economic organization of society. The end and object of capitalist society is the formation and accumulation of surplus value; or in other words, the systematic, legal robbery of the subject working class."

18. Define value and state how measured. [Pg 164]

Ans.: Value is the average amount of human labor time socially, not individually, necessary under average, not special, conditions for the production or reproduction of commodities.

19. What determines the value of labor power?

Ans.: It is determined precisely like the value of every other commodity, i. e., by the amount of labor time socially necessary for its production or reproduction by the raising and support of children to succeed their parents as wage-earning slaves.

20. Since labor power is a commodity, what condition is it subject to?

Ans.: It is subject to the same conditions that all other commodities are subject to without regard to the fact that it is the source of all social value. The worker in whom the commodity labor power is embodied, does not get the value of the product of his labor, but only about one-fifth of it, enough to keep him in working order and reproduce more labor power in his children. If the worker received the value of the product of his labor he would receive much more than enough to keep him in working order and to raise his family. Such an economic condition would abolish all forms of surplus value or profit, also the wage system, by substituting economic and social organization in the interest of the working class. No other class could remain in existence and the class struggle would be ended.

21. In what economic system, past or present, does surplus value appear?

Ans.: It is the root of all social systems since the rise of the institution of private property, but only under the present system (capitalism) has labor power assumed the commodity form. Labor power is a commodity with a two fold character: it has a use and an exchange value. Its use value consists in its being capable of producing values over and above its own needs for sustenance and reproduction. Its exchange value consists in the amount of socially necessary labor time required for its production and reproduction. [Pg 165]

The chattel and feudal systems of slavery were not directly concerned with the production of commodities for the profit of the masters, but rather with the producing of the necessities of life for all, masters and slaves, and the luxuries for some, the masters. That which was not produced for immediate consumption was sold, if opportunities presented themselves, and occasionally the professional traders developed, for example, the Phoenicians; but they were an exception to the rule. The same holds good for feudalism, except that during the latter stages of that system commercialism arose; but this commercialism was no feature of feudalism—it was the rising capitalism that began to unfold and assert itself.

22. Name the three great systems of economic organization upon which the structure of past history and social institutions have their basis.

Ans.: (1) Chattel slavery, (2) serfdom, or feudal slavery and (3) wage slavery.

23. Explain, briefly, how the subject class was exploited under each of these economic systems.

Ans.: 1. Under chattel slavery the laborer was a chattel (possession or property) the same as a mule or horse, and only received his "keep," that is, enough food, clothing and shelter to keep him in working order and to reproduce labor power by raising children. All he produced (use values and children) was taken by his master. The body of the slave was the property of his master. 2. Under serfdom or feudal slavery, the worker produced what was necessary to keep him in working order and to raise a family of slaves, and then the balance of his time produced use values for his feudal lord. The body of the slave was his own, though he could not go about with it from one place to another; for it was bound to the land of his master. 3. Under the wage slavery, the worker receives wages which again equals only the amount necessary to keep him in working order and to reproduce more labor power in his children. His entire product belongs to the capitalist, and out of this resource he pays the wages [Pg 166] for the commodity labor, also for other commodities such as raw materials, and appropriates all of the balance and converts it into capital with which he not only continues but increases the exploitation of his workers. The body of the capitalist's slave is indeed his own as under the feudal system but with this difference, that if he does not like his master, or he is disliked by him, he can or must go abroad with it from one place to another looking for a job—a liberty or necessity which is to the advantage of the owning class and the disadvantage of the working class. Unemployment is necessary to the existence of capitalism, but this necessity is a danger to the system and will ultimately destroy it in all countries as it has in Russia.

24. Define the "Class Struggle."

Ans.: It is the direct clash between two hostile class interests wherein the employing class makes every effort to appropriate more of the wealth produced by the working class, and the working class ever struggles to retain more of the wealth which it produces. The capitalist class strives to get more surplus value and the working class strives to get more wages.

The class consciousness of those who live by working has found one of its best expressions in the following paragraphs:

"The world stands upon the threshold of a new social order. The capitalist system of production and distribution is doomed; capitalist appropriation of labor's product forces the bulk of mankind into wage slavery, throws society into the convulsions of the class struggle, and momentarily threatens to engulf humanity in chaos and disaster.

Since the advent of civilization human society has been divided into classes. Each new form of society has come into being with a definite purpose to fulfill in the progress of the human race. Each has been born, has grown, developed, prospered, become old, outworn, and, has finally been overthrown. Each society has developed within itself the germs of its own destruction as well [Pg 167] as the germs which went to make up the society of the future.

The capitalist system rose during the seventeenth, eighteenth and nineteenth centuries by the overthrow of feudalism. Its great and all-important mission in the development of man was to improve, develop, and concentrate the means of production and distribution, thus creating a system of co-operative production. This work was completed in advanced capitalist countries about the beginning of the 20th century. That moment capitalism had fulfilled its historic mission, and from that moment the capitalist class became a class of parasites.

In the course of human progress mankind has passed (through class rule, private property, and individualism in production and exchange) from the enforced and inevitable want, misery, poverty, and ignorance of savagery and barbarism to the affluence and high productive capacity of civilization. For all practical purposes, co-operative production has now superseded individual production.

Capitalism no longer promotes the greatest good of the greatest number, It no longer spells progress, but reaction. Private production carries with it private ownership of the products. Production is carried on, not to supply the needs of humanity, but for the profit of the individual owner, the company, or the trust. The worker, not receiving the full product of his labor, can not buy back all he produces. The capitalist wastes part in riotous living; the rest must find a foreign market. By the opening of the twentieth century the capitalist world—England, America, Germany, France, Japan, China, etc.—was producing at a mad rate for the world market. A capitalist deadlock of markets brought on in 1914 the capitalist collapse popularly known as the World War. The capitalist world can not extricate itself out of the debris. America today is choking under the weight of her own gold and products.

This situation has brought on the present stage of human misery—starvation, want, cold, disease, pestilence, [Pg 168] and war. This state is brought about in the midst of plenty, when the earth can be made to yield a hundredfold, when the machinery of production is made to multiply human energy and ingenuity by the hundreds. The present state of misery exists solely because the mode of production rebels against the mode of exchange. Private property in the means of life has become a social crime. The land was made by no man; the modern machines are the result of the combined ingenuity of the human race from time immemorial; the land can be made to yield and the machines can be set in motion only by the collective effort of the workers. Progress demands the collective ownership of the land on and the tools with which to produce the necessities of life. The owner of the means of life today partakes of the nature of a highwayman; he stands with his gun before society's temple; it depends upon him whether the million mass may work, earn, eat, and live. The capitalist system of production and exchange must be supplanted if progress is to continue.

In place of the capitalist system we must substitute a system of social ownership of the means of production, industrially administered by the workers, who assume control and direction as well as operation of their industrial affairs."

25. Define "class consciousness."

Ans.: Class consciousness of the workers means that they are conscious of the fact that they, as a class, have interests which are in direct conflict with the interests of the capitalist class.

26. What function does the state perform in the class struggle?

Ans.: "The state is a class instrument, and is the public power of coercion created and maintained in human societies by their division into classes, a power which, being clothed with force, makes laws." It is, therefore, used by the dominant class to keep the subject working class in subjection in accordance with the interests of the ruling and owning class. It is [Pg 169] also used to prevent the workers from altering the economic structure of society in the interests of the working class.

As the author of the catechism, of which these twenty-six questions and answers constitute a small part, says:

"Society is a growth subject to the laws of evolution. When evolution reaches a certain point, revolution becomes necessary in order to break the bonds of the old and bring in the new. As the chicken grows through evolution until it reaches the point where it must break its shell (the revolution) in order to continue its growth, so do classes of people come to the point in their evolution where revolution is necessary in order to continue their growth, bring in the new society and consummate the next step in civilization."

Since 1913, when the foregoing catechism was published, we have had the war to end war and to make the world safe for democracy—a fateful and mournful war in which millions of lives were lost and other millions wrecked with the result of multiplying wars and increasing imperialism.

It was a war between national groups of capitalists with conflicting interests for commercial advantages, which is unexpectedly issuing in three great crises: (1) the imminent bankruptcy of capitalism; (2) the communist revolution in Russia, and (3) the imminent taking over of the world by the revolutionary proletariat.

Hitherto, the sons and daughters of capitalism have owned the earth with all that thereon and therein is. Henceforth, the sons and daughters of the useful workers shall be the owners.

The future belongs to the workers, but not until they organize themselves into one big revolutionary union. What ideas and aims are involved in the faith and endeavor of Revolutionary Unionism will appear from this passage in Comrade Philip Kurinsky's Industrial Unionism and Revolution, a brilliant pamphlet, published by The Union Press, Box 205, Madison Square, New York City: [Pg 170]

"Slavery is not abolished. It is merely a change in the struggle which throws itself hither and thither like the waves of the seas. In ancient times chattel slavery existed. Feudalism then took its place. Feudalism in its turn was overthrown by capitalism which at present reigns supreme. As the immortal Tolstoy explained, 'The abolition of the old slavery is similar to that which Tartars did to their captives. After they had cut up their heels they placed stones and sand in the wounds and then took the chains off. The Tartars were sure that when the feet of their prisoners were swollen, that they could not run away and would have to work even without chains. Such is the slavery of wages'.

Of this slavery does revolutionary unionism speak in the name of the revolutionary worker. It analyzes the present society and shows that it is divided into two economic classes. One class, the capitalist class, is the master class which controls all the factories, mills, mines, railroads, lands and fields and all the finished and raw materials. This class possesses all the natural riches of the world and this economic supremacy gives it control of the state, of the church, and of all educational institutions. In short, this class owns everything and controls the whole social and political life of each country. The other class, the working class, owns nothing. It produces all and enjoys little. It uses the machines and tools but does not possess them, and is therefore forced to sell its only possession, its labor power, to the master class. And the latter uses the opportunity to buy that wonderful power like any raw material or some other commodity (some of the representatives of craft unionism wish to deny this but unsuccessfully). For the commodity which the worker is compelled to sell in order that he might live, he receives a wage which is determined as is the price of every other commodity. The price is always smaller than the value of the product which the worker produces for the capitalist.

Between these two classes there must, naturally, [Pg 171] exist a tremendous struggle which often has the character of actual war. No one urges the workers to this war—not the terrible I. W. W.'s nor the political socialist, neither the Bolsheviks nor the Anarchists, but the war naturally and inevitably arises from existing conditions.

On the one hand, the capitalists are continually chasing after higher profits which results in the employment of cheap labor under the worst conditions. Naturally the ideal of the capitalist class is to keep the workers in a condition of slavery. If the workers attempt to revolt, as they do daily, their masters try to suppress the revolt with all the power at their command. On the other hand, the workers struggle with all their power to lighten their burdens. They strive to get better conditions, higher wages and shorter hours, and in general the ideal of the working class is to throw off the yoke of capitalism.

No one rightfully can say that this struggle is merely a theory. We can see this struggle in the attempts of the capitalist class to destroy the victorious Russian Proletariat. It is mirrored before our eyes in the continual strikes. Nothing can stop this struggle except the abolition of exploitation.

No matter how hard the Citizens' Committees, Boards of Arbitration, of Conciliation and of Mediation, with their so-called impartial members try to convince the world that it is possible to bring the warring classes into closer relations, their attempts are doomed to failure. At best their success is only temporary and their efforts succeed only in blinding the eyes of the working masses. And if at some time these boards claim a victory, the credit is not due to them, but to the force exerted by the workers. It is the strike-weapon, held in reserve by the toilers, that brings victory to the workers—not the efforts of the philanthropic gentlemen. Furthermore the efforts of these gentlemen greatly harm the workers, for at times when the workers can attain success through the use of the strike, these philanthropists interfere, and deaden [Pg 172] the initiative and aggressiveness of the strikers. Often this causes strife between the strikers themselves. They lose confidence in one another, and the existence of the organizations which the workers succeeded in building up through their efforts and sacrifices are jeopardized.

The "Conciliation," however, can bring no conciliation between the employers and workers, because that is unnatural. On the contrary, the hatred of one side to the other is intensified and war breaks out oftener and assumes a more bitter and more obstinate character.

Thus viewing the two struggling classes of capitalist society, revolutionary industrial unionism comes to the logical conclusion that between capital and labor there exists nothing in common, that the struggle must go on and peace can come only when economic oppression will cease, which is possible only when the program of revolutionary unionism will be realized; namely, when the workers will take over the means of production and abolish the system of private ownership. The autocratic control of industry, the unequal division of products will then disappear and society will be built on a socialist foundation, where the industries will be owned and operated by the workers, organized in a truly democratic manner, and where the individual will receive the full product of his labor.

These are the principles of revolutionary unionism, the principles of the international proletariat. They are the true expressions of the class struggle and because of that, revolutionary unionism attracts more and more followers whose ideal is to develop within the working masses a consciousness of their historic mission."

In the words of an eloquent representative of the organized workers in the United States, I exhort the working men and working women of America: Keep your eyes on Russia. Watch what is going on there and what the capitalist plunderbund will try to do.

Do not be misled by the lies and slanders that are daily dished [Pg 173] up to you. Bear in mind that those who tell you these yarns have an interest to mislead you. They want to use you as a make-weight in their game of wresting from the Russian workers their dearly-won liberty. It is of no use to enumerate the lies that have already been punctured because they will invent new ones faster than one can write and print. Let your reason guide you. Think yourselves into the shoes of your Russian fellow workers. Think how you would act if placed in the same position and then draw the conclusion that they act about the same way that you would, because they are like you moved by the same emotions, the same desires, the same aspirations. You, too, would like to keep for yourselves the fruits of your toil, if you only knew how to go about it, if you had the organization that would make it possible. But as yet you do not know and you have not that organization. In politics you still vote against one another in the Republican or Democratic camp. You will have to wait until you do know and until you do have the means—the Industrial Unions of the entire working class that will be able to take and hold and administer industry for the reason that it will have the might, the power to do so. And when you have expressed through the ballot your will for that new society, which will guarantee to you the full fruits of your labor, remember the slogan of revolutionary Russia: "All power to the Soviets," and let your slogan then be: "All power to the Industrial Unions!"

These are prophetic words written fifty years ago by Frederick Engels:

Since the historical appearance of the capitalist mode of production, the appropriation by society of all the means of production has often been dreamed of, more or less vaguely, by individuals, as well as by sects, as the ideal of the future. But it could become possible, could become a historical necessity, only when the actual conditions for its realization were there. Like every other social advance, it becomes practicable, not by men understanding that the existence of classes is in contradiction to justice, equality, etc., not by the mere will [Pg 174] ingness to abolish these classes, but by virtue of certain new economic conditions.... So long as the total social labor only yields a produce which but slightly exceeds that barely necessary for the existence of all; so long, therefore, as labor engages all or almost all the time of the great majority of the members of society—so long, of necessity, this society is divided into classes....

But if, upon this showing, division into classes has a certain historical justification, it has this only for a given period, only under given social conditions. It was based on the insufficiency of production. It will be swept away by the complete development of modern productive forces. And, in fact, the abolition of classes in society presupposes a degree of historical evolution, at which the existence, not simply of this or that particular ruling class, but of any ruling class at all, has become an obsolete anachronism....

With the seizing of the means of production by society, production of commodities is done away with, and, simultaneously, the mastery of the product over the producer. Anarchy in social production is replaced by systematic, definite organization. The struggle for individual existence disappears. Then for the first time man, in a certain sense, is finally marked off from the rest of the animal kingdom, and emerges from mere animal conditions into really human ones.... It is the ascent of man from the kingdom of necessity to the kingdom of freedom.

The capitalist countries are ruled through banks, and a bank is necessarily an institution of the owning class.

Russia is ruled through Soviets, and a soviet is necessarily an institution of the working class.

Banks and Soviets are so many headquarters for big unions. In capitalist countries the banks are such for the one big union of the owners, and in Russia the soviets are this for the one big union of the workers. These big unions cannot co-exist and flourish in the same country. [Pg 175]

All owners everywhere see the necessity for their one big union and in all capitalistic countries, nowhere more than in the United States, they have the advantage of being on the ground floor and indeed on all the floors of all the sky scrapers with their union which is the most universally inclusive and the most relentlessly efficient organization on earth.

Some workers everywhere see the necessity for their one big union, but nowhere is it seen as generally and clearly as in Russia,—

the only country in which the workers have held the ground floor for any considerable time against all comers.

In all countries a beginning has been made by the workers in laying the foundation for their one big union, but in only one country, Russia, has progress been made with the superstructure, and here as everywhere the owners have hindered the workers so that they must defend themselves with their right hand while they build with their left. Nevertheless wonderful progress is being made and when the industrial structure has been completed, as it soon must be, else the world is doomed to destruction, it shall tower above its capitalist rival as a mountain over a foot hill.

After all, the power of the owner is money and it is not a real potentiality, for within the social realm there is in reality only one potentiality, the power of productivity which exclusively belongs to the worker.

In the sky there is no god, and on earth there is no king or priest like unto Labor, the lord of gods, the tzar of kings and the pope of priests.

Labor is high above all potentialities. The motto, "All Power to the Workers," which the class-conscious proletarians inscribe on their banners, is not the expression of an ideal fiction, but the declaration of a practical reality, the greatest among all realities, that reality in which the whole social realm lives, moves and has its being.

Down with the one big union of the owners. Long live the one big union of the workers.

[Pg 176]

II. GOD AND IMMORTALITY.

> We have done with the kisses that sting, With the thief's mouth red from the feast, With the blood on the hands of the king, And the lie on the lips of the priest.
> —Swinburne.

Many critics contend that socialism and supernaturalism are not, as I represent, incompatibilities; but they lose sight of four facts: (1)

this is a scientific age; (2) Marxian socialism is one of the sciences; (3) the vast majority of men of science reject all supernaturalism, including of course the gods and devils with their heavens and hells, and (4) only in the case of one of the sciences, psychology, is this majority greater than in the science of sociology.

The truth of the last two of these representations will be overwhelmingly evident from the chart on the next page. It and its explanation given in the following quotation is taken with the kind consent of the author and also of the publishers of a book entitled God and Immortality, by Professor James H. Leuba, the Psychologist of Bryn Mawr College. This book is having a great influence and I strongly recommend it to all who think that I am wrong in the contention that conscious, personal existence is limited to earth; that, therefore, we are having all that we shall ever know of heaven and hell, here and now, and that whether we have more of heaven and less of hell depends altogether upon men and women, not at all upon gods and devils. The second edition of Professor Leuba's book is now in the press of The Open Court Publishing Company, 122 South Michigan Ave., Chicago, Ill. Here is the quotation in support of our contentions: [Pg 177]

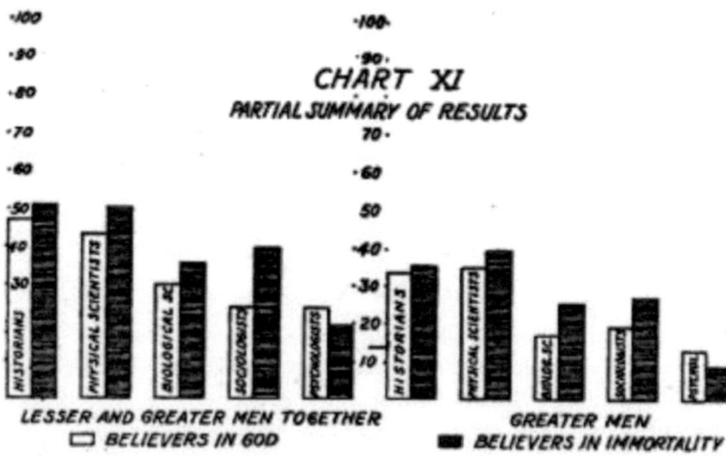

[Pg 178]

What, then, is the main outcome of this research? Chart XI, Partial Summary of Results, shows that in every class of persons investigated, the number of believers in God is less, and in most classes very much less than the number of non-believers, and that the number of believers in immortality is somewhat larger than in a personal God; that among the more distinguished, unbelief is very much more frequent than among the less distinguished; and finally that not only the degree of ability, but also the kind of knowledge possessed, is significantly related to the rejection of these beliefs.

The correlation shown, without exception, in every one of our groups between eminence and disbelief appears to me of momentous significance. In three of these groups (biologists, historians, and psychologists) the number of believers among the men of greater distinction is only half, or less than half the number of believers among the less distinguished men. I do not see any way to avoid the conclusion that disbelief in a personal God and in personal immortality is directly proportional to abilities making for success in the sciences in question.

A study of the several charts of this work with regard to the kind of knowledge which favors disbelief shows that the historians and the physical scientists provide the greater; and the psychologists, the sociologists and the biologists, the smaller number of believers. The explanation I have offered is that psychologists, sociologists, and biologists in very large numbers have come to recognize fixed orderliness in organic and psychic life, and not merely in inorganic existence; while frequently physical scientists have recognized the presence of invariable law in the inorganic world only. The belief in a personal God as defined for the purpose of our investigation is, therefore, less often possible to students of psychic and of organic life than to physical scientists.

The place occupied by the historians next to the physical scientists would indicate that for the present the reign of law is not so clearly revealed in the events with which history deals as in biology, economics, and psy [Pg 179] chology. A large number of historians continue to see the hand of God in human affairs. The influence, destructive of Christian beliefs, attributed in this interpretation to more intimate knowledge of organic and psychic life, appears incontrovertibly, as far as psychic life is concerned, in the remarkable fact that whereas in every other group the number of believers in immortality is greater than that in God, among the psychologists the reverse is true; the number of believers in immortality among the greater psychologists sinks to 8.8 per cent. One may affirm it seems that, in general, the greater the ability of the psychologist, the more difficult it becomes for him to believe in the continuation of individual life after bodily death.

Within the generation to which I belong Darwin and Marx, the greatest teachers that the world has had, went over the top of entrenched ignorance with the greatest books of the world, worth infinitely more to it than all its bibles together. Darwin did this in 1859 with his Origin of Species by Natural Selection and Marx in 1867 with his Capital, a Critique of Political Economy.

Darwin with his book is driving the Christian church out of its trench of supernaturalism and uniqueism by showing that the different kinds of vegetable and animal life are not, according to the representation of its bible, so many separate creations by a personal, conscious divinity, but interrelated evolutions by an impersonal, unconscious nature, the higher out of the lower, and that, therefore, man is so far from being a special creation, having his most vital relationships with a celestial divinity and his most glorious prospects in a heavenly place with him, that he is really more or less closely related to every [Pg 180] living thing on earth, and is as hopelessly limited to it, as an elephant, a tree or even a mountain.

Marx with his book is driving the states out of the trench of imperialism and capitalism.

As Darwin is driving the conscious, personal gods out of the realm of biology, placing all animal and human life of body, mind and soul on essentially the same footing, so Marx is driving all such divinities out of the realm of sociology, placing all life of family, state, church, lodge, store and shop on essentially the same level.

According to Darwin, all animal life is what it is at any time by reason of the effort to accommodate the physical organism to its environment.

According to Marx, human civilization is what it is at any time because of the economic system by which people feed, clothe and house themselves.

This Darwinian-Marxian interpretation of terrestrial life in general, and of the human part of it in particular, is known as materialism. It is the materialistic, naturalistic, levelistic interpretation of history, and differs fundamentally from the spiritualistic, supernaturalistic, uniqueistic interpretation of Christian preachers. The contrast between these interpretations is especially strong in the case of human history.

On the one hand the Christian preacher says, man's history is what it is because of the directing providence of a God, the Father, Son and Spirit, and because of His directing inspiration of great leaders, such as Washington, Luther, Caesar and Moses.

On the other hand Darwin and Marx agree in saying that both the triune god and the inspired leader [Pg 181] are what they are, because society is what it is; that, again, the character of society depends upon the economic system by which it feeds, clothes and houses itself, and that finally all such systems owe their existence to the machinery in use for the production of the basic necessities of life, the primal machine being the human hand to which all other machines are auxiliaries.

The most insatiable and universal among all human longings is for freedom—freedom from economic want, social inequality and imperialistic tyranny, also freedom to learn, think, live and teach truths.

Socialism of the Marxian type is the gospel of freedom, because a classless god, nature, reveals it in the interest of a classless world: therefore, it is true, and slavery, of which there never was so much before on the earth, and nowhere is there more than in the United States, is utterly incompatible with truth, and classless interests.

All the supernaturalistic gospels are revealed by a class god (Jesus, Jehovah, Allah, Buddha) in the interest of the capitalist class: therefore, they are false and freedom is utterly incompatible with falsehood and class interest.

Ignorance is the destroyer-god and capitalism is the diabolical scourge by which he afflicts the wage-earner with many unnecessary sufferings, especially the crushing ones arising from the great trinity of evils, war, poverty and slavery.

Knowledge is the saviour-god and Marxism is his divine gospel of freedom from these capitalistic sufferings. [Pg 182]

III. MYTHICAL CHARACTER OF OLD AND NEW TESTAMENT PERSONAGES.

What man of sense will agree with the statement that the first, second, and third days, in which the evening is named and the morning, were without sun, moon and stars? What man is found such an idiot as to suppose that God planted trees in Paradise like an husbandman? I believe that every man must hold these things for images under which a hidden sense is concealed.—Origen.

One of the critics of Communism and Christianism whose representations are in alignment with several others says:

While the Bishop speaks in the language of scholarship, he entirely ignores all the findings of modern scholars on the literature of the Bible.

The failure to show more clearly that my representations concerning the untenableness of the basic doctrines of Christian supernaturalism are in alignment with the conclusions of outstanding authorities in the newly developed sciences of historical and biblical criticisms is indeed a defect and an attempt will here be made to remove it by a short but faithful and, as I think, convincing summary of what such authorities in these sciences have to say on the subject.

My summary is summarized from a pamphlet by Charles T. Gorham, published by Watts and Company, 17 Johnson's Court, Fleet St., E. C. 4, London, England, which is itself an able summarization of the relevant facts which have been scientifically established as they are given in the greatest of all the Bible Dictionaries, the Encyclopedia Biblica.

It will be seen that all except one among my contentions concerning the baselessness of the supernaturalism of orthodox Christians are well sustained. This [Pg 183] exception is the contention that Jesus is not an historical personage, but a fictitious one. However the great critics are unanimously with me even in this, for two crushing facts are admitted by them: (1) the Old Testament affords no scientifically established data from which a reliable history of the

Jews can be written, and (2) the New Testament has no such data for a biography of Jesus.

The illuminating summary which is a large part of my answer to the criticism under review follows, and it is as far as possible in the language of Mr. Gorham:

Once upon a time there was a system of Christian Theology. It was a wonderful though a highly artificial structure, composed of fine old crusted dogmas which no one could prove, but very few dared to dispute. There was the "magnified man" in the sky, the Infallible Bible, dictated by the Holy Spirit, the Trinity, the Fall, the Atonement, Predestination and Grace, Justification by Faith, a Chosen People, a practically omnipotent Devil, myriads of Evil Spirits, an eternity of bliss to be obtained for nothing, and endless torment for those who did not avail themselves of the offer.

Now the house of cards has tumbled to pieces, or rather it is slowly dissolving, as Shakespeare says, "like the baseless fabric of a vision". The Biblical chronology, history, ethics, all are alike found to be defective and doubtful. Divine Revelation has become discredited; a Human Record takes its place. What has brought about this startling change? The answer is, Knowledge. Thought, research, criticism, have shown that the traditional theories of the Bible can no longer be maintained. The logic of facts has confirmed the reasonings of the independent thinker, and placed the dogmatist in a dilemma which grows ever more acute. The result is not pleasant for the believer; but it is well that the real state of things should be known, that the kernel of truth should be separated from the overgrown husk of tradition.

[Pg 184]

During the last few years a work has been issued which sums up the conclusions of modern criticism better than any other book. It is called the Encyclopedia Biblica, and its four volumes tersely and ably set forth the new views, and support them by a mass of learning which deserves serious consideration. And the most significant thing about it is not merely that the entire doctrinal system of Christianity has undergone a radical change, but that this change has largely been brought about by Christian scholars themselves. A rapid glance at this store-house of the heresy of such scholars will give the reader some idea of the extent of the surrender which Christianity has made to the forces of Rationalism. It must be premised that space will permit of the conclusions only being given, without the detailed evidence by which they are supported.

Let us begin with our supposed first parents. Is the story of Adam and Eve a true story? There are, we are told, decisive reasons why we cannot regard it as historical, and probably the writer himself never supposed he was relating history. [K]

The Creation story originated in a stock of primitive myths common to the Semitic races, and passed through a long period of development before it was incorporated in the book of Genesis. If, then, it is the fact, as Christian scholars assert, that this story of the Creation originated in a pagan myth, and was shaped and altered by unknown hands for nearly a thousand years, it is nothing more nor less than superstition to hold that it is divinely true.

As for the Old Testament patriarchs, we now learn that their very existence is uncertain. The tradition concerning Abraham is, as it stands, inadmissible; he is not so much a historical personage as an ideal type of character, whose actual existence is as doubtful as that [Pg 185] of other heroes. All the stories of the patriarchs are legendary.

The whole book of Genesis, in fact, is not history at all, as we understand history. Exodus is another composite legend which has long been mistaken for history.

The historical character of Moses has not been established, and it is doubtful whether the name is that of an individual or that of a clan. The story of his being exposed in an ark of bulrushes is a myth probably derived from the similar and much earlier myth of Sargon. [L]

Turning to the New Testament, we find that modern critical research only brings out more clearly than ever the extraordinary vagueness and uncertainty which enshroud every detail of the narrative. From the article on "Chronology" we learn that everything in the Gospels is too uncertain to be accepted as historical fact. There are numerous questions which it is "wholly impossible to decide". We do not know when Jesus was born, or when he died, or who was his father, or what was the duration of his ministry. As these are matters on which the Gospel writers purport to give information, the fact of their failure to do so settles the question of their competency as historians.

The supposed supernatural birth of Jesus has of late exercised the minds of theologians. It is not surprising that some of them should reject the notion, for it is one without a shred of evidence in its favor. Setting aside the well-known fact that many other religions assume a similar origin for their founders, we may note the New Testament accounts are in such hopeless conflict with each other that reconciliation is impossible.

The important subject of the "Resurrection" is treated by Professor P. W. Schmiedel, of Zurich, who tells us that the Gospel accounts "exhibit contradictions of the most glaring kind". [Pg 186]

The article on the Gospels by Dr. E. A. Abbott and Professor Schmiedel is crammed with criticism of a kind most damaging to every form of the orthodox faith. The view hitherto current, that the four Gospels were written by Matthew, Mark, Luke, and John, and appeared thirty or forty years after the death of Jesus, can, it is stated, no longer be maintained.

The alleged eclipse of the sun at the Crucifixion is impossible. One of the orthodox shifts respecting this phenomenon is that it was an eclipse of the moon!

Modern criticism decides that no confidence whatever can be placed in the reliability of the Gospels as historical narratives, or in the chronology of the events which they relate. It may even seem to justify a doubt whether any credible elements at all are to be found in them. Yet it is believed that some such credible elements do exist. Five passages prove by their character that Jesus was a real person, and that we have some trustworthy facts about him. These passages are: Matthew xii. 31, Mark x. 17, Mark iii. 21, Mark xiii. 32, and Mark xv. 34, and the corresponding passage in Matthew xxvii. 46, though these last two are not found in Luke. Four other passages have a high degree of probability—viz., Mark viii. 12, Mark vi. 5, Mark viii. 14-21, and Matthew xi. 5, with the corresponding passage in Luke vii. 22. These texts, however, disclose nothing of a supernatural character. They merely prove that in Jesus we have to do with a completely human being, and that the divine is to be sought in him only in the form in which it is capable of being found in all men. [M]

The four Gospels were compiled from earlier materials [Pg 187] which have perished, and the dates when they first appeared in their present form are given as follows:—Mark, certainly after the destruction of Jerusalem in the year 70; Matthew, about 119 A. D.; Luke, between 100 and 110; and John, between 132 and 140.

The question of the genuineness of the Pauline Epistles, is now far from being so clear as was once universally supposed. Advanced criticism, Professor Van Manen tells us in his elaborate article on "Paul", has learned to recognize that none of these Epistles are by him, not even the four generally regarded as unassailable. They are not letters to individuals, but books or pamphlets emanating from a particular school. We know little, in reality, of the facts of Paul's life, or of his death: all is uncertain. The unmistakable traces of late origin indicate that the Epistles probably did not appear till the second century.

The strange book of Revelation is not of purely Christian origin. Criticism has clearly shown that it can no longer be regarded as a literary unit, but it is an admixture of Jewish with Christian ideas and speculations. Ancient testimony, that of Papias in particular, assumed the Presbyter John, and not the Apostle, as its author or redactor.

The Epistles of Peter, James and Jude are none of them held to be the work of the Apostles. They probably first saw the light in the second century; the second Epistle of Peter may even belong to the latter half of that period.

All the above conclusions are summarized, as nearly as may be, in the words of the authors of the respective articles. Their significance is surely enormous. Right or wrong, eminent Christian scholars here proclaim results in complete antagonism to the ideas usually accepted as forming the true basis of the Christian faith. They amount, in fact, to a complete and unconditional surrender of the whole dogmatic framework which has hitherto been held as divinely revealed, and therefore divinely true. [Pg 188]

Thomas Paine was a Deist. As such he believed that nature may be compared with a clock and God with its maker. As the clock maker, under normal conditions, has but little to do with his handiwork, so it has been with the Creator and his universe. The theists of every name (Christian, Jew, Mohammedan and Buddhist), not to speak of others, believe that the universe, with all which therein is, lives, moves and has its being as the result of the willings of their respective gods.

Though I have my god, indeed two gods, one god in the world of my physical existence—a trinity: matter, force and motion, and another god in the world of my moral existence—a trinity: fact, truth and life, yet if the rejection of both deism and theism is atheism, I am an atheist.

But assuming for the sake of argument that there is a conscious personal being who has had and is having something to do with making things what they are, I set my seal to this arraignment:

Of all the systems of religion that were ever invented, there is none more derogatory to the Almighty, more unedifying to man, more repugnant to reason, and more contradictory in itself, than this thing called Christianity. Too absurd for belief, too impossible to convince, and too inconsistent for practice, it renders the heart torpid, or produces only atheists and fanatics. As an engine of power, it serves the purpose of despotism and as a means of wealth, the avarice of priests; but for the good of mankind it leads to nothing here or hereafter.

—Thomas Paine.

William Rathbone Greg in his Creed of Christendom says that much of the Old Testament which Christian divines, in their ignorance of Jewish lore, [Pg 189] have insisted on receiving and interpreting literally, the informed Rabbis never dreamed of regarding as anything but allegorical. The literalists they called fools.

Origen and Augustine, the two greatest men which Christianity has produced, would agree with Greg in this. We have already quoted the motto of this section from Origen, and we will now quote this from Augustine:

It very often happens that there is some question as to the earth or the sky, or the other elements of this world, respecting which one who is not a Christian has knowledge derived from most certain reasoning or observation, and it is very disgraceful and mischievous and of all things to be carefully avoided, that a Christian, speaking of such matters as being according to the Christian Scriptures, should be heard by an unbeliever talking such nonsense that the unbeliever, perceiving him to be as wide from the mark as east from west, can hardly restrain himself from laughing.

FOOTNOTES:

[K] But if Adam and Eve are not historical personages there is no doctrine of supernaturalistic Christianism resting on the solid ground of facts and the whole of its immense dogmatic structure is floating in the air of theories and myths.—Author.

[L] It is questionable whether such persons as Samson, Jonah and Daniel ever lived, but it is certain that their adventures are as mythical as anything in Aesop's Fables.—Author.

[M] But these nine texts which for some years were often triumphantly pointed to as the pillars upon which securely rested the historicalness of Jesus as a man are now lying in the dust where the learned and brilliant Professor William Benjamin Smith of Tulane University put them by his great contribution to the Christological problem in a book, entitled Ecce Deus in which he, as I think, proves conclusively that the Jesus of the New Testament never was a real man but always an imaginary god, the Christian recasting of the Jewish God, a new Jehovah.—Author.

IV. WOULD SOCIALISM CHANGE HUMAN NATURE?

> Fear not the tyrants shall rule for ever, Or the priests of the bloody Faith: They stand on the brink of that mighty river Whose waves they have tainted with death, It is fed from the depths of a thousand dells, Around them it foams and rages and swells, And their swords and their scepters I floating see Like wrecks in the surge of eternity.
> —Shelley.

My revolt against the existing capitalist system of economics and the capitalized political and religious systems which support it is complete, and the end [Pg 190] which I have in view in this booklet is that of primitive Christianism, as it is taught by Mary in the Magnificat, the putting down of the owning masters of the world and the exaltation of the working slaves, only that I do not recommend, as she did, that the masters should be banished to starve but rather that they should be allowed to become producers and to live then as such, not as robbers, as they now live.

This is bolshevism. It is not anarchy, but a new dictatorship instead of the old, that of the proletariat in place of the bourgeoisie. But this dictatorship (though necessary during the period of transition from the capitalist system, by which commodities are made only for the profit of a few to an industrial system by which they will be made only for use of the many) is not the goal of socialism. Its goal is a classless world—a world in which all who are able to work shall directly or at least indirectly contribute their due proportion, according to their abilities and opportunities, towards feeding, clothing, housing and educating it.

Perhaps the truest thing in the Bible relates to the utterly corrupt condition of civilization, nor was it ever truer than now, and it always must be equally true while the world is divided into master and slave classes under the dictatorship of the masters:

The whole head is sick and the whole heart faint. From the sole of the foot even unto the head, there is no soundness in it, but wounds and bruises, and putrifying sores: they have not been closed, neither bound up, neither mollified with ointment.

Capitalism and Socialism differ fundamentally in that the former always has sought and always will [Pg 191] seek to exercise a permanent dictatorship, whereas that of the latter is to constitute the temporary bridge over which the world is to pass from the economic system under which commodities are competitively made for the profit of the few, to the economic system under which they will be co-operatively made for the use of the many.

It is contended with much show of reason that the dictatorship of the proletariat will not lead to the goal, because human nature being what it is the slaves will automatically develop into another class of masters.

But those who raise this contention proceed upon the assumption that human nature is a constant quantity so that it cannot be essentially changed and that it has made the economic systems, what they have been.

This is not the case. Human nature, like animal nature, is constantly changing and neither the one nor the other voluntarily changes itself, but both are forced to change by the development of new and external conditions and by the necessity of conformity to them.

Professor Joseph McCabe, not a socialist, observes that these developments and conformities were so many revolutions and that the man who says, the secret of progress is evolution, not revolution, may be talking very good social philosophy but he is not talking science, as he thinks. In every modern geological work you read of periodical revolutions in the story of the earth, and these are the great ages of progress—and, I ought to add, of colossal annihilation of the less fit.

Darwin discovered that animal nature changed (for [Pg 192] example snake nature changed into bird nature) because of changed physical environments and the necessity of life to adaptation to them.

Marx discovered that human nature changed from what it was during the period of chatteldom to what it was during serfdom and from that to what it is under capitalism by reason of the difference in the economic systems of these periods by which the world fed, clothed and housed itself and that these differences are in turn accounted for by the differences in the machines by which the necessities of life are produced.

Thus Darwin explained the history of animal life without the hypothesis of a divine creator, and Marx explained the history of mankind without the hypothesis either of a divine ruler or human leaders. These Darwinian and Marxian explanations constitute what is known as the materialistic explanation of history.

Marx represented that capitalism would end the class struggle and issue in a classless world because its profiteering system of production and distribution could not be succeeded by another, since it divides mankind into masters who are ever growing less numerous and slaves who are ever growing more numerous, without the possibility of those who are half capitalists and half workers rising out of their nondescript condition into a new master class, as did the bourgeoisie under feudalism. For these reasons he contended the proletarian slaves would become the grave diggers for the bourgeois masters and so end capitalism with the burial of its representatives.

But with the complete and sustained triumph of the proletarian class the bourgeois class will rapidly pass away, as is now the case with it in Russia, and a class [Pg 193] less world will be born to live on a co-operative instead of a competitive basis, in a heaven instead of a hell.

V. WHAT WILL BE THE FORM OF THE WORKERS' STATE.

Hail Soviet Russia, the first Communist Republic, the land of, by and for the common people. We greet you, workers and peasants of Russia, who by your untold sacrifices, by your determination and devotion, are transforming the Russia of black reaction, of the domination of a few, into a land of glorious promise for all. Comrades in America, watch the bright dawn in the East; you have but your chains to lose, and a world to gain!—The Workers' Council.

In general outline the form of the workers' state will be that of the Russian Soviet Republic, and what it is will appear from the following semi-official description, the briefest and clearest of any which I have seen. Its authorship is unknown to me but I know it to be the work of a committee of which Zinoviev, one of the directing and inspiring minds of the proletarian movement in Russia, was a member, and it may be that he is the author. Anyhow it is a recently published, authoritative classic containing the information for which a large part of the world has been waiting:

We have before us the example of the Russian Soviet Republic, whose structure, in view of the conflicting reports printed in other countries, it may be useful to describe briefly here.

The unit of government is the local Soviet, or Council, of Workers', Red Army, and Peasants' Deputies.

The city Workers' Soviet is made up as follows: Each factory elects one delegate for a certain number of workers, and each local union also elects delegates [Pg 194] . These delegates are elected according to political parties—or, if the workers wish it, as individual candidates.

The Red Army delegates are chosen by military units.

For the peasants, each village has its local Soviet, which sends delegates to the Township Soviet, which in turn elects to the County Soviet, and this to the Provincial Soviet.

Nobody who employs labor for profit can vote.

Every six months the City and Provincial Soviets elect delegates to the All-Russian Congress of Soviets, which is the supreme governing body of the country. This Congress decides upon the policies which are to govern the country for six months, and then elects a Central Executive Committee of two hundred, which is to carry out these policies. The Congress also elects the Cabinet—The Council of People's Commissars, who are heads of Government Departments—or People's Commissariats.

The People's Commissars can be recalled at any time by the Central Executive Committee. The members of all Soviets can be recalled very easily, and at any time, by their constituents.

These Soviets are not only Legislative bodies, but also Executive organs. Unlike your Congress, they do not make the laws and leave them to the President to carry out, but the members carry out the laws themselves; and there is no Supreme Court to say whether or not these laws are "constitutional."

Between the All-Russian Congresses of Soviets the Central Executive Committee is the supreme power in Russia. It meets at least every two months, and in the meanwhile, the Council of People's Commissars directs the country, while the members of the Central

Executive Committee go to work in the various government departments.

In Russia the workers are organized in Industrial Unions all the workers in each industry belonging to one Union. For example, in a factory making metal products, even the carpenters and painters are members [Pg 195] of the Metal Workers' Union. Each factory is a local Union, and the Shop Committee elected by the workers is its Executive Committee.

The All-Russian Central Executive Committee of the federated Unions is elected by the annual Trade Union Convention. A Scale Committee elected by the Convention fixes the wages of all categories of workers.

With very few exceptions, all important factories in Russia have been nationalized, and are now the property of all the workers in common. The business of the Unions is therefore no longer to fight the capitalists, but to run industry.

Hand in hand with the Unions works the Department of Labor of the Soviet Government, whose chief is the People's Commissar of Labor, elected by the Soviet Congress with the approval of the Unions.

In charge of the economic life of the country is the elected Supreme Council of People's Economy, divided into departments, such as, Metal Department, Chemical Department, etc., each one headed by experts and workers, appointed, with the approval of the Union by the Supreme Council of People's Economy.

In each factory production is carried on by a committee consisting of three members: a representative of the Shop Committee of the Unions, a representative of the Central Executive of the Unions, and a representative of the Supreme Council of People's Economy.

The Unions are thus a branch of the government—and this government is the most highly centralized government that exists.

It is also the most democratic government in history. For all the organs of government are in constant touch with the working masses, and constantly sensitive to their will. Moreover, the local Soviets all over Russia have complete autonomy to manage their own local affairs, provided they carry out the national policies laid down by the Soviet Congress. Also, the Soviet Government represents only the workers, and cannot help but act in the workers' interests.

[Pg 196]

The motto of this section is the conclusion of a good article in the first number of one among the best of the periodicals devoted to the promotion of Marxism, The Workers' Council, published by the International Educational Company, New York City. This article is so short and lends itself so naturally as a supplement to the foregoing explanation of the new economic system which has been established and is being developed in Russia that I quote the rest as the conclusion of this section about Sovietism.

Communist Russia, the Russia of the common people, marks a new epoch in the world's history. It marks a basic change in the structure of human society. Up to this time society lived under the rule of the few, under the rule of the class which possessed the wealth of the country. The methods were different at different periods in the world's history, but the results were the same: riches and power for the few, a bare existence and endless toil for the many. The slaves, the serfs, or the wage workers of today, who compose the masses of the people, have ever been the hewers of wood and the carriers of water, the beasts of burden on whose backs sported and fattened kings and nobles, landlords and capitalists. They who possessed wealth had the power. And they passed laws to protect that power, to make the possession of wealth a social institution. Private property was enthroned and every striving of mankind was subjected to the rule of property. Thence grew the exploitation of man by man for private profit, and all abuses resulting therefrom; fear of loss of property, care of possession, dread of the future, fear of loss of employment, envy and greed. Human society was ruled by property grabbers; masters, kings, capitalists, providing toil, disease, war for the masses of mankind. That is the rule of capitalism, and cannot be otherwise.

But under communism, profit is abolished, and with it the exploitation of man by man; private property is [Pg 197] no longer a factor in the life of man; property becomes universal, all natural and created wealth belong to society, to every member of the community, as secure a birth right as air and sunlight. Everybody's measured work provides a common fund of things to satisfy material needs, today, tomorrow and in years to come. There can be no fear of losing one's job, of seeing one's children starve, of the poor-house in old age. As sure as the sun will rise on the morrow, man is secure of his bread, his shelter and clothing. Man is freed from animal cares, free to develop his human qualities, his intelligence, his brain and heart.

Russia points the way. Russia is now one huge corporation, every man, woman and child an equal shareholder. The state is administered as a business; the benefit of the stockholders being the object of the corporation. The individual contributes his labor, whatever it may be: manual, mental, artistic. This labor is applied to available materials: the soil of the farm, the natural resources, the mines, and mills and factories. The finished product is distributed through the agencies of the corporation, in the shape of food and clothes and shelter, of education and amusement, of protection to life and limb, of literature and art, of inventions and improvements: to every man, woman and child of the nation.

To be sure this ideal of a human brotherhood is not yet realized in Russia. No sane person would expect so tremendous a change to be consummated in three years, in the face of universal aggression, intrigues and blockades. It may take ten years, perhaps a generation. What of it! Russia is past the most difficult period of transition from the capitalist state to a communist state, while other capitalist countries must still face the period of revolution. Therefore let Russia lead the way. Let the American workers realize that Russia's fight is their fight, that Soviet Russia's success is the success of the laboring people the world over! [Pg 198]

> Have you ever been to Crazy Land, [N] Down on the Looney Pike? There are the queerest people there— You never saw the like! The ones that do the useful work Are poor as poor can be, And those who do no useful work All live in luxury. They raise so much in Crazy Land Of food and clothes and such, That those who work don't have enough Because they raise too much. They're wrong side to in Crazy Land, They're upside down with care— They walk around upon their heads, With feet up in the air.

—T.

VI. WITHDRAWAL OF PRIZE OFFER.

Never have anything to do with those who pretend to have dealings with the supernatural. If you allow supernaturalism to get a foothold in your country the result will be a dreadful calamity.—Confucius.

Mrs. Brown and I hereby withdraw, for the present at least, our prize offer, and for two reasons:

1. We are convinced that it is as necessary to the welfare of the world to smite supernaturalism in religion as capitalism in politics, but while many are able and willing to attack the octopus of capitalism, this is true of only a few in the case of the dragon of supernaturalism. Some hesitate because they feel with one of the critics of Communism and Christianism that revolutionary forces are coming to the surface in the churches. [Pg 199]

"Where," he asks, "shall we classify the stand of the Catholic Church against the open shop? What shall be said of the Interchurch report on the steel strike? What of the attitude of the combined commission in Denver of Catholics, Protestants and Jews on the street car strike?"

We have no desire to belittle such efforts nor to discourage their promoters; but (though they may afford some local and temporary alleviation to the miseries of far the greater part of the world—miseries growing out of its division into two classes, a small class of owning masters and a large class of working slaves) we center no hope in them, because the whole history of the supernaturalistic interpretations of religion, not excepting the Christian, show these efforts to be only reformatory and temporary bubbles which sooner or later are always pricked by the masters of what little revolutionary air they contain, and so never issue in any general or permanent improvement of the sad lot of the overwhelming majority of the slaves.

How little the church serves the working slaves, and how much the owning masters, will appear from the following representations of Roger W. Babson, the well-known financial expert and adviser:

The value of our investments depends not on the strength of our banks, but rather upon the strength of our churches. The underpaid preachers of the nation are the men upon whom we really are depending, rather than the well-paid lawyers, bankers and brokers. The religion of the community is really the bulwark of our investments. And when we consider that only 15 per cent of the people hold securities of any kind and less than 3 per cent hold enough to pay an income tax, the importance of the churches becomes even more evident. [Pg 200]

For our sakes, for our children's sakes, for the nation's sake, let us business men get behind the churches and their preachers. Never mind if they are not perfect. Never mind if their theology is out of date. This only means that were they efficient they would do very much more. The safety of all we have is due to the churches, even in their present inefficient and inactive state. By all that we hold dear, let us from this very day give more time, money and thought to the churches, for upon these the value of all we own ultimately depends.

What our critics say about the recent efforts of the American churches being in the right direction is interesting to Mrs. Brown and me, but we are much more impressed by the observation of a writer in a late issue of Soviet Russia. In speaking of the baneful influence of the Russian church through all the ages he says:

Out of the shadows of antiquity, from the morning of man's cupidity and avarice, two sinister figures have crawled with crooked talons through history, leaving a trail of blood and fear most horrible which has not halted yet. These are the monarch and the priest. The one is symbolical of despotic or oligarchic power, the other typifies the sordid ignorance and fearful superstition of the credulous masses which maintains the power of the first. High in the streets of Moscow, where one may see the pallid, long-haired, degenerate-looking venders of holy lies and pious impositions shuffle along like spectres from a remoter age, there hangs a woven streamer of scarlet hue with huge white lettering, which defiantly proclaims that religion is the opium of the people.

Though many still cross themselves a score of times daily on passing the church, yet nevertheless the people are rapidly assimilating the knowledge which elevates and enlightens, and learning to reject that which terrorizes and deforms the mind, and just so sure as the [Pg 201] last filthy tyrant has been placed for ever beyond mischief, so will the last priest soon vanish from the land once contemptuously known as "Holy Russia".

The foregoing is from a revolutionary sympathizer with soviet Russia and the following is from a reactionary criticizer of it, but both are to the same effect, that orthodox Christianity is wholly against the interest of the proletariat and entirely for that of the bourgeoisie:

One of the most striking characteristics of Bolshevism is its pronounced hatred of religion, and of Christianity most of all. To the Bolshevik, Christianity is not merely the theory of a mode of life different from his own; it is an enemy to be persecuted and wiped out of existence.

To understand this is not difficult. The tendency of the Christian religion to hold before the believer an ideal of a life beyond death is diametrically opposed to the ideal of Bolshevism, which tempts the masses by promising the immediate realization of the earthly paradise. From that point of view Christianity is not only a false conception of life; it is an obstacle to the realization of the Communist ideal. It detaches souls from the objects of sense and diverts them from the struggle to get the good things of this life. According to the Bolshevist formula, religion is opium for the people: and serves as a tool of capitalist domination.

This influence of the churches, in the long run and on the whole has been and will continue to be the same throughout christendom everywhere and everywhen, not excepting these United States in the twentieth century.

Nor is it to any convincing purpose that the representatives of the owning class contend that kings and priests have lost their supremacy to presidents and [Pg 202] preachers, for it is imperialism in politics which enthralls and supernaturalism in religion which degrades. The world is greatly afflicted with both, none of it much, if any, more than our country.

It seems to us that we see two fundamentally important facts more clearly than our critics see them: (1) the first step in the way of salvation for the proletariat is class consciousness, and (2) the Christian interpretation of supernaturalistic religion has been, and until it is discredited will continue to be the most efficient among the many preventives to this consciousness.

Let me show this to be the case by an experience which I had some years ago when Mr. Pierpont Morgan, Senior, was at the height of his glory, as the king of the great realm of big business, receiving homage on the one hand from the Rockefellers and Rothschilds, and on the other hand from the Blockheads and Henry Dubbs of all the world.

At that time I made a confirmation visitation for my sick episcopal brother, the Bishop of New York, to what was popularly known as Pierpont Morgan's church (St. George's, one of the downtown churches for working people.) He was the senior warden of this great parish having nearly 5,000 communicants. He went with the collecting procession out through the great congregation and back to the chancel where each collector ceremoniously emptied the contents of his basket into the great gold alms basin held by the Rector.

While the famous financier was collecting contributions from obscure toilers, how could any, brought up as I was and as nearly all of the great [Pg 203] congregation were, see that capitalism has divided humanity into two conflicting classes which "have nothing in common, the working class and the employing class, between which a struggle must go on until the workers organize, take possession of the earth and the machinery of production and abolish the wage system!"

By the light of what I had been taught all along and of what I was then seeing with my own eyes from the bishop's chair such a representation would have seemed preposterous and what was true of me was equally so of all present, rector, wardens, vestrymen, members and visitors.

There were not many I. W. W.'s. in those days, but if one had been there and upon leaving the church had made a representation to this effect to a fellow-worker who was a member of St. George's would not the reply have been something as follows:

See what Pierpont Morgan and I have in common: the same God; the same religion; the same church; the same services for worship; the same collection basket in which he puts a $100.00 bill and I a ten cent piece; the same Lord's Supper where we eat and drink together; and, besides all this, there is the same hell where he will go unless he gives me a fair day's wage and where I will go unless I do a fair day's work, and the same heaven where both will go to equally glorious mansions, if we are alike 100 percenters in church and state, and if he pays me liberally for my work and I slave hard enough for his money.

Assuming the truth of the Christian interpretation of religion this conclusion is correct. But this Chris [Pg 204] tian religion is not true. Christianism offers nothing to either the owners or workers in the sky for its god and heaven, devil and hell are lies. And neither religious Christianism nor political Republicanism or Democracy, not to speak of the other isms of religion and politics, offers the workers aught on earth.

Capitalism is the god of this world, of no part of it more than of these United States, and capitalism is to the laborer a robbing, lying, murderous devil, not a good divinity.

2. The recall of the prize offer is also occasioned and justified, we think, by a demand, which was as unexpected as it is gratifying, for our little propagandist in foreign countries, and we have been persuaded that it should be met by securing to him the gift of tongues. We propose to do this by devoting the money which was set aside for the prizes to the encouragement of making and publishing translations.

FOOTNOTES:

[N] The capitalist countries of the world constitute the United States of Crazy Lands.

VII. AFTERWORD.

> "So many Gods, so many Creeds, So many ways that wind and wind, When all this sad world really needs Is just the art of being kind."
> —Ella Wheeler Wilcox.

I.

My title, given in Latin on the picture page, is bestowed upon me by some in jest and by others in reproach, and I am accepting it from both as compliments, because they prove that I have at least succeeded in making clear the general outlines of my religious and political position. [Pg 205]

The use of this title is due to the desire that those who pick up the booklet should not buy it, much less undertake to read it, under a mistaken impression as to its doctrinal trends. In English the Latin title is, "Bishop of the Countries belonging to the Bolsheviki and the Infidels."

Certain friends greatly fear that some things said in this booklet may fall foul of the criminal-syndicalism laws. I have carefully read those of Ohio and believe that the booklet contains nothing which is not safely within them.

Anyhow, I have spoken the truth about supernaturalistic religion and capitalistic politics as I understand it, and I believe that I have adequately supported all my representations on bases of relevant facts which cannot be gainsaid or, at any rate, upon sound arguments which have such facts for their foundations.

However, I am trying to hold myself open to conviction; and, this being the case, if "the powers that be" in state or church feel that they must proceed against me, I beg that, in justice to all the persons and interests concerned, they will come with their resources of persuasion, not coercion.

My appeal to the religious and political rulers to do this shall be in the burning words of a celebrated defender of the capitalistic system of economics, John Stuart Mill, words which constitute the most remarkable passage in his powerful essay on Liberty:

No argument, we may suppose, can now be needed, against permitting a legislature or an executive, not identified in interest with the people, to prescribe opinions to them, and determine what doctrines or what arguments they shall be allowed to hear. [Pg 206]

Speaking generally, it is not, in constitutional countries, to be apprehended, that the government, whether completely responsible to the people or not, will often attempt to control the expression of opinion, except when in doing so it makes itself the organ of the general intolerance of the public.

Let us suppose, therefore, that the government is entirely at one with the people, and never thinks of exerting any power of coercion unless in agreement with what it conceives to be their voice.

But I deny the right of the people to exercise such coercion, either by themselves or by their government. The power itself is illegitimate. The best government has no more title to it than the worst. It is as noxious, or more noxious, when exerted in accordance with public opinion, than when in opposition to it.

If all mankind minus one, were of one opinion, and only one person were of the contrary opinion, mankind would be no more justified in silencing that one person, than he, if he had the power, would be justified in silencing mankind.

Were an opinion a personal possession of no value except to the owner; if to be obstructed in the enjoyment of it were simply a private injury, it would make some difference whether the injury was inflicted on only a few persons or on many. But the peculiar evil of silencing the expression of an opinion is, that it is robbing the human race; posterity as well as the existing generation; those who dissent from the opinion, still more than those who hold it. If the opinion is right, they are deprived of the opportunity of exchanging error for truth: if wrong, they lose, what is almost as great a benefit, the clearer perception and livelier impression of truth, produced by its collision with error.

This passage should be inscribed in letters of gold on the doors of every church and court house in [Pg 207] the world. It was written in condemnation of the persecution by majorities of minorities in states, but it applies equally to all intolerance of dissentient o-pinions.

It is utterly impossible in a printed discussion of the length of this booklet to weed out every word capable of misconstruction; and equally so to furnish a definition or limitation to every doubtful word or phrase. Nevertheless I call attention to a few:

The word "revolution" as used here should not be taken as implying armed insurrection or violence, unless expressly so described. These are not necessary features of revolution. There have been both political and industrial revolutions entirely unattended by violence or bloodshed; for example, the political revolution of 1787 when the old Articles of Confederation were abolished and the federal Constitution imposed upon the United States; also the political and industrial revolution of 1919 in Hungary when for a time a soviet system was established, with Bela Kun as premier.

The bloodshed which often attends revolutions comes almost invariably from the lawless counter-revolutionary efforts of the deposed ruling class to maintain themselves in power or regain power by terrorism and murder.

When I eulogize the Bolsheviki and their system in Russia, I am not to be taken as advocating for the United States the employment of the bloody tactics for gaining power, which the capitalist press of America persists in describing—and as I believe, falsely. I deal in this booklet not with tactics but with facts. I concern myself here not with the ways [Pg 208] by which the Bolsheviki of Russia gained power, but with what they did with the power after gaining it.

As I was trained in theology, I am certain that my religious position has been so clearly outlined that no mistake as to where I stand will be made by the rulers in my church; but, having had no training in the law, I am less certain that my political position will be as unmistakably understood by the rulers in my state. Therefore, to avoid misinterpretation of certain words and phrases in this booklet, I here expressly disclaim any intention of violating the criminal-syndicalism statute of Ohio, following as closely as may be its phraseology in these my denials of criminal intention:

Nothing herein is to be understood as advocating or teaching the duty, necessity, or propriety of crime, sabotage, violence or unlawful methods of terrorism as a means of accomplishing industrial or political reform. This booklet is not issued for the purpose of advocating, advising, or teaching the doctrine that industrial or political reform should be brought about by crime, sabotage, violence or unlawful methods of terrorism; nor of justifying the commission or the attempt to commit crime, sabotage, violence or unlawful methods of terrorism with intent to exemplify, spread or advocate the propriety of the doctrines of criminal syndicalism; nor of organizing any society, group or assemblage of persons formed to teach or advocate the doctrines of criminal syndicalism. If any such meaning shall be read into any passage of this booklet by any reader, it will be a wrong meaning, not what I intended to convey.

[Pg 209]

A revolution by which a new industrial democracy—the freedom to make things for the use of workers—will supplant the old capitalist democracy—the freedom to make things for the profit of owners—is an inevitable event in the history of every country within the twentieth century.

II.

My object in this booklet is not the promotion of class hatred and strife. Far from it. It is to persuade to the banishment of gods from skies and capitalists from earth.

Theism and capitalism are the great blights upon mankind, the fatal ones to which it owes, more than to all others together, the greatest and most unnecessary of its suffering, those arising from ignorance, war, poverty and slavery.

This recommendation as to banishments and this representation in support of it stand out on nearly every page of the booklet, and in order to make sure of special prominence for them on its last pages, I quote the following from an article by G. O. Warren (a major in the British army, I think) an occasional contributor of brilliant articles to rationalist publications on sociological lines:

If there be a God who rules men and things by His arbitrary will, it is an impertinence to attempt to abolish poverty, because it is according to His will. But if there be no such God, then we know that poverty is caused by men and may be removed by men. If there be a God who answers prayers, the remedy for social injustice is to pray. But if there be no such God, the remedy is to think and act.

If men go to heaven when they die, and if heaven [Pg 210] is a place in which everybody will be made perfectly happy, then there is no need to struggle against poverty in this world, because a few years of trouble, or even degradation, in this world are of no consequence when compared with an eternity of happiness that must be ours by simply following the directions of the clergy. But if there be no such heaven, then it becomes a matter of first importance that we make our condition as happy as possible in this world, which is the only one of which we are certain.

I maintain that there is no God who rules men and things by His arbitrary will and who answers prayers, and that there is no heaven of everlasting bliss to which we are to be wafted after death. And I maintain this not only because I think that these religious beliefs are erroneous, but because I know that they are most potent to make men docile and submissive to the most degrading conditions imposed on them. I feel sure that the doctrine that obedience to rulers and contentment in poverty are according to the will of God, and the doctrine that the poor and the oppressed will be compensated in heaven are the chief causes of slums, prisons, lunatic asylums and poor-houses.

All political tyranny is backed up and made possible by belief in an arbitrary God, and all poverty is endured because of the belief that after death everlasting happiness and wealth await us. Two conditions are necessary to human happiness: personal freedom and general wealth. But we never can be free as long as we believe that it is the will of an infinite heavenly ruler that we should submit to a finite earthly ruler, whether he gets upon the throne by hereditary succession or by the votes of a majority; and wealth will never be justly, and therefore, generally, distributed as long as most of the people believe that because they are poor in this world they will be rich in the world to come.

The apostle Paul says that political rulers are ordained by God and must be obeyed, from the King to the constable, from the President to the policeman. [Pg 211] He says that if you are refractory, "the minister of God" will use his sword, and will not use it "in vain." He says that the sword-bearer is God's minister.

Christ himself recites a parable about a rich man who went to hell because he was rich and a poor man who went to heaven because he was poor. Rich Christians are told by the clergy that the surest way for them to get to heaven is by being rich; but they use this parable to console the poor with the idea that the surest way for them to get to heaven is by being poor. And this idea is confirmed by the saying of Christ: 'Blessed are the poor, for theirs is the kingdom of heaven.'

I claim that it is impossible to prove that any being exists who can do, or ever does, anything outside of the regular processes of Nature, and therefore that the word "God," which has always meant such a being, should be dropped. I would have no objection to the current use of the word "God" if that use were harmless, but it is very far from that. It is a word that every despot conjures with to keep the people in ignorance and subjection. It is a word that crafty politicians use in carrying out their schemes of bribery and plunder.

The same thing applies to the word "heaven." It is impossible to show that there is any such place, and the word is used as a bribe to the poor to keep them quiet under injustice. I do not see how there can be a life after death, but if there is it will not be any better because we are poor and undeveloped in this world, and therefore immortality should be a reason rather for discontentment among the poor than for submission to injustice.

As an atheist, I object to a God who is for every tyrannical ruler and against the rebels that he imprisons, tortures and slays; who is for the idle landlord and usurer and against the workers; who is for the purse-proud prelate and against the people; who is for the boodle politician and against the happiness [Pg 212] of the many; who is for the white exploiter and against the simple colored man; who is for the rich profiteer and against the petty burglar and pickpocket.

If I am told there is no such God as this, I reply that there is, or there is none. The God of every Christian creed is the God of the rulers, the God of the idle rich. There never has been any other God known to the world. This is the God that the church now worships and always has worshiped.

There are forces in Nature that we do not yet understand, and therefore should not name. But they can only help us as we learn what they are and how to use them. It is therefore neither our duty nor our privilege to pray, nor can any good be thus achieved. It is for us to observe, to think, and to examine the pretensions of the privileged. It is for us to understand that there is no God to raise our wages, and no heaven to compensate us for our poverty and all the misery it entails in this world.

> "Said the parson, 'Be content; Pay your tithes due, pay your rent; They that earthly things despise Shall have mansions in the skies, Though your back with toil be bent,' Said the parson, 'be content.'
> "Then the parson feasting went With my lord who lives by rent; And the parson laughed elate For my lord has livings great, They that earthly things revere May get bishop's mansions here.
> "Be content! Be content! Till your dreary life is spent, Lowly live and lowly die, All for mansions in the sky! Castles here are much too rare, All may have them—in the air!"

[Pg 213]

III.

According to Marxian socialism, the history of man arose from the need of his body for food, raiment and shelter. This is the materialistic explanation of history, and the following is one of the passages in which Marx clearly shows that it is true and reasonable:

In the social production which men carry on they enter into definite relations that are indispensable and independent of their will; these relations of production correspond to a definite stage of development of their material powers of production. The sum total of these relations of production constitutes the economic structure of society—the real foundations, on which rise legal and political superstructures and which correspond to definite forms of social consciousness. The mode of production in material life determines the general character of the social, political and spiritual processes of life. It is not the consciousness of men that determines their existence but, on the contrary, their social existence determines their consciousness. At a certain stage of their development, the material forces of production in society come in conflict with the existing relations of production, or—what is but a legal expression for the same thing—with the property relations within which they had been at work before. From forms of development of the forces of production these relations turn into their fetters. Then comes the period of social revolution.

Marx and his followers are justified in their contention that the physical necessities of man (not gods or great men) constitute the key to his history by the fact that there was no mind of man before the human body nor will there be any mind when the body has been disintegrated; for the mind was made by the body, for the [Pg 214] body, not the body by the mind, for the mind. This very remarkable fact, when duly considered, will change nearly all the ideas of most men and women about almost everything.

A leader is but a mouthpiece of a people through which they give expression to their deepest convictions and highest aspirations. Early in my life Lincoln was the great leader of the people in the United States, and late in it Lenin is the great leader of the people of the world. The earlier of these was at least a rationalist and the latter is an atheist, so that the first probably did not suppose himself to have been inspired by a divinity, and the second certainly does not.

I claim, said Lincoln, not to have controlled events, but confess plainly that events have controlled me.

In Lenin's Birthday Anniversary number of the magazine, Soviet Russia, the Editor says:

At the very outset, we must clearly state that much of Lenin's powerful position in present-day history is made by the history itself,—by the fact that we are living at the moment when the entire life of the race is vindicating in a most emphatic manner the theoretical position occupied by Lenin for many years. After all, Lenin, like Trotsky, was an unknown man, except to certain political circles, and the mass of Russian revolutionists, even as late as 1916. And yet, he was the same Lenin; had not the opportunity come to put into practice the system for which he and his associates had been laboring and suffering for many years, no doubt the circle of his admirers and readers would not be much wider in 1920 than it was in 1916. Lenin would probably be the first to admit—nay, insist—that the material circumstance that enables a certain individual to assert himself is the prime element in building his reputation. So that, [Pg 215] if the Russian Revolution had not taken the course it did take, Lenin, with exactly the same mental and idealogical preparation, might have remained a relatively unknown man.

Those who on the one hand interpret life from the naturalistic or materialistic point of view, and those who on the other hand interpret it from the supernaturalistic viewpoint need not and generally do not differ as widely as is commonly supposed.

Materialism is the name for two totally different things, which are constantly confused. There is, in the first place, materialism as a theory of the universe—the theory that matter is the source and the substance of all things. That is (if you associate "force" or "energy" or "motion" with your "matter," as every materialist does) a perfectly arguable theory. It has not the remotest connection with the amount of wine a man drinks or the integrity of his life.

But we also give the name of materialism to a certain disposition of the sentiments, which few of us admire, and which would kill the root of progress if it became general. It is the disposition to despise ideals and higher thought, to confine one's desires to selfish and sensual pleasure and material advancement. There is no connection between this materialism of the heart and that of the head.

For whole centuries of Christian history whole nations believed abundantly in spirits without it having the least influence on their morals; and, on the other hand, materialists like Ludwig Buchner, or Vogt, or Moleschott, were idealists (in the moral sense) of the highest order. Look around you and see whether the belief or nonbelief (for the Agnostic is in the same predicament here) in spirit is a dividing-line in conduct. There is no ground in fact for the confusion, and it has wrought infinite mischief.—McCabe.

[Pg 216]

As to their philosophy concerning the origin, sustenance and governance of the universe, communists are almost to a man materialists; but, as to their philosophy concerning life, they are as generally idealists. There is, I feel sure, as much idealism in my thinking and living now as there was in the days of my orthodoxy.

Many of the representations of the Jewish-Christian Bible are materialistic in a high, if not gross, degree. This is true of the account of the creation according to which the god, Jehovah, with hands moulded a man out of dust; performed a surgical operation upon him for the purpose of securing a rib out of which he carved a woman; made a garden; and provided worship for himself by a system of material sacrifices. The ark of the covenant was a wooden chest, and its contents (a pot, some manna, and Aaron's rod) were materialities.

The conception, birth, death, descension, resurrection, ascension and session of the god, Jesus, were (if they occurred) material realities. And the eating of the flesh and drinking of the blood of the god sounds like materialism, especially according to the explanation of the Greek, Roman, Lutheran and Anglican churches.

IV.

A nutshell summary of this booklet is contained in these confessions of my religious and political faith:

I. My religious faith is summed up in the following creed of twelve Articles:

(1) The chief end of every man should be to make the most of his own life by having it as long and as happy as possible and to help others in doing this for themselves. [Pg 217]

(2) Though parents live unconsciously in their children and all do so in those over whom they have had any influence, yet all there is of conscious, personal life for man is of a terrestrial character, none celestial.

(3) Knowledge is the Christ of the World. The saviour-gods of the supernaturalistic interpretations of religion are symbols of this one.

(4) Ignorance is the devil of the world. The destroyer-gods of the supernaturalistic interpretations of religion are symbols of this one.

(5) Knowledge consists in knowing facts and truths. Every real fact and truth is a word of the only gospel which the world possesses.

(6) A fact is something which matter, force and motion have unconsciously done, not what a god has consciously willed. There are no other facts.

(7) A truth is a fact so interpreted that if it is lived it will contribute towards making the most of life. There are no other truths.

(8) Hence the greatest people in the world are the scientists who discover facts, and the preachers who interpret them and persuade to their living. If you contend that mothers are greater than teachers, I shall agree with you on condition that you will admit that a mother is not really great unless she is a teacher.

(9) The desire and effort to learn facts, interpret and live them constitute morality.

(10) Morality is the greatest thing in the world, because it is all there is of real religion and politics.

(11) But, paradoxical as it may seem, there is one thing which is greater than the greatest thing in the world—freedom. [Pg 218]

(12) And the freedom which is greater than morality consists in the liberty to learn, interpret, live and teach facts, without which liberty a man may be a non-moral child, or an immoral hypocrite, but he cannot be the possessor of the pearl of great price—morality, without which human life is not worth the living or even possible.

II. My political faith is summed up in the following creed of twelve articles:

(1) As the universe in general is self-existing, self-sustaining and self-governing, so man in particular, who is but one among the transitory, cosmic phenomena, has all of the potentialities of his own life within himself, so that every man can say of himself what the makers of Jesus had him say: I and my Father are one.

(2) Man has set a far-off and high-up goal of an ideal civilization for himself, and is finding the way to it by his own discoveries, and is walking therein by his own strength, so that he is not in the least indebted to any of the gods of the supernaturalistic interpretations of religion, either for the setting of the goal, or for what progress he has made towards it.

(3) Nor is humanity indebted to its outstanding representatives for the advance in the way of civilization, as is evident from the fact that, but for the gods, it would have long since been far beyond the point where the English-German war would have been within the range of possibilities, and these gods are the gifts to a blind humanity by its blind leaders.

(4) Humanity is not indebted to its physical scientists any more than to its spiritual prophets for its advance in the way of civilization, because the scientists [Pg 219] have always worked, as the prophets have preached, in the interests of the profiteers of the existing system of economics. Economic systems have been the chief, if not indeed, the only promoters of war, and the world war with its tremendous horrors would not have been possible but for science.

(5) So, then, the history of civilization has been what it is because of the economic systems by which the material necessities of life (foods, raiments and houses) have been produced, not because gods have made spiritual revelations, nor yet because men have made great discoveries and persuasively taught them. According to Marx, who discovered the key to the door of history, it is constituted neither by the gods in the skies, nor the great men on earth; but by economic systems. These create the divinities and the leaders, not they them.

(6) Thus far in the history of mankind every civilization has rested upon the institution of slavery and there have been, speaking broadly, three different forms of it, with their correspondingly different civilizations, chattel, feudal and capital. Each of these forms of slavery has been the foundation for a superstructure of a civilization peculiar to a distinct period of history. Chattel, feudal and capital slaveries respectively constituted the foundations for the superstructures of ancient, mediaeval and modern civilizations. The second of the two great discoveries by Marx was that the wage sla-

very of capitalism, by far the worst of all slaveries, is due to surplus profits.

(7) Since civilizations have their embodiments in religious and political institutions (churches and states with what goes with them) so clearly as to justify the [Pg 220] contention that religion and politics are the halves of one and the same reality—civilization—it follows that I am right in carrying my materialism over from the realm of religion into that of politics.

(8) A system of economics is about the most materialistic thing in the world, yet it is the only key which will open the door to the temple of human history. Having opened it with this key, the first thing to be seen is a world divided into two classes, one class whose representatives live by owning the material means and the machines for production and distribution; and another class whose representatives live by working in making and operating these machines, with the result of producing and distributing the material commodities by which the world is fed, clothed and housed, but to the surfeiting of the owners who as such produce nothing and have everything and the starving of the workers who produce everything and have nothing.

(9) Capitalists and communists agree that when the goal of humanity has been reached the world will find itself to be one all inclusive co-operating family.

(10) Capitalists say that then the co-operating will be between the owners as fathers, and the workers as children. The capitalists will recognize every laborer who does a fair day's work as a good son or daughter, and the laborer will recognize every owner who gives a fair day's wage as a good father.

(11) But communists say that then the co-operating will be between men, all of whom are on the same footing as laborers, since, when the goal is reached, the world will no longer be divided as it has been, from time out of mind, into a small owning or master class and a large working or slave class; but it will consti [Pg 221] tute one great all inclusive family, every member of which will be on the same footing with all others, except that the older members will regard the younger as sons and daughters, and they in turn will

be regarded as fathers and mothers, and all of the same generation will look upon each other as brothers and sisters.

(12) Civilization always has been and ever will be impossible without slavery, because leisure and opportunity for study, social intercourse and travel are necessary to it, but under capitalism, as it works out, only representatives of the owning or master class have these prerequisites, and those of the working or slave class must be deprived of them. When communism supplants capitalism all will have their equal parts in both the labor necessary to the sustenance of the physical (body) life, and also the leisure necessary to the development of the psychical (soul) life. There will still be slavery, indeed much more of it than the world has hitherto known, but machines, not men, women and children will be the slaves. Of course there will remain much work connected with the making and operating of the machines, but the time and energy required for it will more and more decrease with the inevitable increase in the number and efficiency of the machines until, according to conservative estimates, three or four hours per day of comparatively light and pleasant employment will be quite sufficient to provide the necessities of life in abundance for every worker and his dependents, so that, then, all will have as much of them as the few have now; and this without any sense of slavery because when one is working for the benefit of himself and his own in particular, and the public to which he belongs [Pg 222] in general, not for the profit of a class of which he is not a representative, there is no feeling of irksome servitude.

V.

A world-wide revolution has begun and is rapidly spreading over the earth. Why? Because a world-wide economic system for feeding, clothing and housing the people has broken down so that it must be supplanted by a new system, else mankind will perish for the lack of food, raiment and shelter.

This revolutionary war is between the working class whose representatives live starvingly, though they produce and distribute all the necessities of life and the capitalist class whose representatives live surfeitingly, though taking no part in the production and distribution of these necessities.

Nearly one hundred years ago our fourth President, James Madison, saw partly and dimly what nearly every one now sees fully and clearly:

We are free today substantially, but the day will come when our Republic will be an impossibility. It will be an impossibility because wealth will be concentrated in the hands of a few. A republic cannot stand upon bayonets, and when that day comes, when the wealth of the nation will be in the hands of a few, then we must rely upon the wisdom of the best elements in the country to readjust the laws of the nation to the changed conditions.

The laborers of Russia have turned the country right side up so that they themselves are above and the capitalists below, having the privilege of remaining down to idle and starve or else to crawl up to work and live, but not to rob, war and enslave. [Pg 223]

As I lay down my pen the working man's government of Russia is fighting a double war, the Poland-Crimea war, to prevent its overthrow by the capitalist governments of the world, especially England, France, Japan and the United States, which in this war are surreptitiously confederated against it, and the victory seems assured to it, largely because of the sympathy and help of their fellow workers throughout the world.

Marx though dead yet speaketh. He is speaking more widely and persuasively in death than in life. Russia is the megaphone from which his voice goes out through every land and over every sea.

Never man nor god spake with as much power as he speaks. His gospel is to the slave, and this is its thrilling appeal—workers of the world unite, and this is its inspiring assurance—you have nothing to lose but your chains and a world to gain.

WM. M. BROWN.

Brownella Cottage, Galion, Ohio.
September 24th, 1920.